Douglas B. Bailey

life Spirals

The FAITH JOURNEY

Iris M. Ford

D0830242

WELCH PUBLISHING COMPANY INC.
Burlington, Ontario, Canada

To the congregation of
Waterloo North Presbyterian Church,
always encouraging in our shared ministry.
Together we have grown in faith.

ISBN: 1-55011-075-6

© 1988 by Iris M. Ford

Welch Publishing Company Inc.
960 The Gateway
Burlington, Ontario
L7L 5K7 Canada

Printed in Canada

CONTENTS

FOREWORD

There is a growing interest in the concept of *faith development* among religious professionals, both in Canada and the United States. It has been stimulated in good measure by the emerging awareness of developmental patterns of adulthood, which in turn has motivated a more specialized form of awareness among those who work in the area of adult spirituality.

James Fowler's research, and his resulting conceptualization of a comprehensive theory of faith development (*Stages of Faith*, 1981), has provided the central focus for interest in the field. For that matter, Fowler's impact has been so strong that professionals sometimes refer to his stages as "stages" of faith development. In many ways this is unfortunate, since it precludes the exploration of the other models for describing the faith journey.

In *LIFE SPIRALS: The Faith Journey*, Iris Ford provides another model. She helps us to expand our understanding of the nature of faith development. She brings together, in a new way, several important elements in the developmental journey of faith to provide a deeper understanding of the concept.

1. She integrates faith development theory, based on Fowler, with the psychosocial developmental concepts of Erikson, and has done so with fresh insight.

2. She illustrates this interplay with the striking conceptualization of a Spiral Faith Model, which brings new dimensions to what is often expressed as a linear progression. Even the graphic model she presents cannot do justice to the Spiral Faith Model: I have in my study a *three-dimensional* model of the Spiral, given to me by Iris, which provides vibrant representation of the faith steps.

3. Of most importance, she illustrates the model with the faith journey of an individual, a real person — herself. She shares with us, intimately yet appropriately, some of the joys and sorrows, successes and stumbles that have been a part of her life — and faith — journey. This openness not only illustrates a theory; it invites each of us to explore more fully *our own* life journey of faith.

The Spiral Model will touch many of us in ways that more academic works cannot. It helps the religious professional bridge the gap between theory and practice in ministry. It helps the lay member of a church, parish, or synagogue relate the ritual and practices of the faith community to his or her own faith life. It helps the searching person who is not part of a faith community find meaning for his or her faith within or outside such a community.

LIFE SPIRALS: The Faith Journey is an important new book. It moves us another step closer to understanding the self in the journey of faith. Thank you, Iris, for helping many of us take this step in our lives.

Kenneth Stokes
Executive Director
Adult Faith Resources
9709 Rich Road
Minneapolis, Minnesota, 55437

PREFACE

This book is written for people who are wondering about their faith and have doubts. It probably shows a Western, Christian bias, but I have no apologies for that, as this book is based on my own experiences with the faith journey. I can only be what I am. I hope, though, that its circulation will not be limited to churches, but will be read by people in general. Perhaps they will dig into these pages and use the ideas to figure out something interesting and exciting about their own faith journey.

For some, faith may seem irrelevant. Perhaps there are few changes evident in their lives which are attributable to "faith." But what is faith? Faith here is not just "religious faith," though that is included. Nor is faith just trust in oneself or in another person or goal. Faith is our response to everything that calls a person to open up and grow. It is the spiritual discovery that there is more to life than is currently realized, and reaching for it. Faith is openness to life!

A second book, currently being written, will trace how Biblical concepts have informed the Spiral Faith Model presented here. It would be interesting also to share this model with people of other world religions, and with those who profess to be non-religious. Surely faith, as presented here, is a universal human response to life itself.

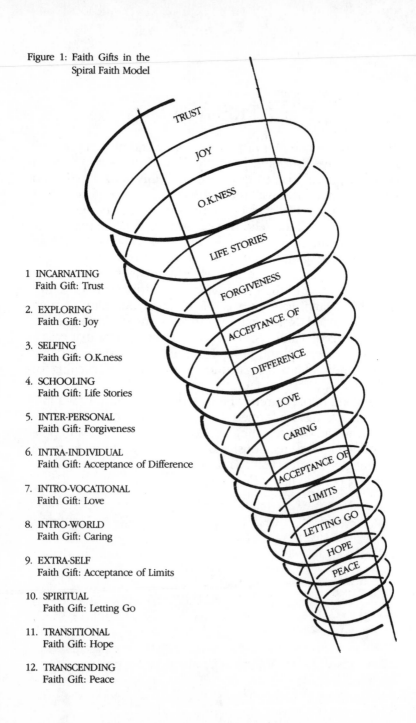

Figure 1: Faith Gifts in the
Spiral Faith Model

TRUST

JOY

O.K.NESS

LIFE STORIES

FORGIVENESS

ACCEPTANCE OF

DIFFERENCE

LOVE

CARING

ACCEPTANCE OF

LIMITS

LETTING GO

HOPE

PEACE

1 INCARNATING
Faith Gift: Trust

2. EXPLORING
Faith Gift: Joy

3. SELFING
Faith Gift: O.K.ness

4. SCHOOLING
Faith Gift: Life Stories

5. INTER-PERSONAL
Faith Gift: Forgiveness

6. INTRA-INDIVIDUAL
Faith Gift: Acceptance of Difference

7. INTRO-VOCATIONAL
Faith Gift: Love

8. INTRO-WORLD
Faith Gift: Caring

9. EXTRA-SELF
Faith Gift: Acceptance of Limits

10. SPIRITUAL
Faith Gift: Letting Go

11. TRANSITIONAL
Faith Gift: Hope

12. TRANSCENDING
Faith Gift: Peace

INTRODUCTION

My eyes were caught and held spellbound! There in the corner of my friend's living room was a beautiful fluorescent lantern, with bright red spirals circling round. It drew me, speaking to me of life. There didn't seem to be any deliberate order in the spirals; they were just all in motion, appearing, pulsing, turning. No one spiral dominated for long, but in its brief moment each caught my attention. This spiral lantern drew my heart. It suggested to me that spirals could be an intriguing symbol for growth in faith, with each spiral representing part of life itself.

Use of a spiral model for growth suggests that human growth is cyclic and ongoing. Growth is dependent on the past, illuminates the present, and points to the future. Spirals suggest that all of life's challenges keep repeating themselves at ever-deepening levels, calling a person to grow and expand. As a model for the faith journey, spirals suggest that faith is cyclic, and ever-expanding, constantly calling a person to grow.

One day, while having an afternoon nap, I had a strange dream. I was looking out the front door in a thunderstorm when lightning flashed right overhead and hit me. I knew I was dying and said, "Oh God, I'm coming to you, please help me." It was as if I were being sizzled and time stood still. I awoke suddenly, surprised to find that I was safe in my bed! The dream was so real it was startling and I wondered what influence caused it.

Just before going to sleep I had been reading an article in *Reader's Digest* on aging. In doing the questionnaire I had assessed my projected death at age 84. So I went to sleep thinking about death and wondering if I was ready. Did the dream reflect reality in my life? Do I not fear death? How deep does faith go into the dream state? How does it grow in a person?

My purpose in writing this book is to try to understand how

11

people grow in faith. There are many more questions ahead:

What is faith?
Is it a journey, a process?
Are there identifiable parts?
Is there a definable, even predictable growth pattern?
Is there enough similarity among humans to suggest stages in faith development?
Is growth in faith sequential, dependent on what was previously experienced?
What does faith reach for?

Christianity has influenced my faith search, but surely faith as a human response is possible for all, regardless of particular religious practices, or lack of religion. However, while a simple faith, in the sense of the human response, is possible for everyone, transcendent faith is not that simple. Transcendent faith is beyond the temporal, beyond the self's control, beyond the person's response.

In writing this book, I have wondered about my personal faith journey and so I have included it here. Perhaps my story will illustrate some of the spirals in the faith model, so others can identify them as they think about their own unique faith journey. I am single, female, and living in relative ease in Ontario, Canada. Being in my middle fifties, I can look back over the years and ahead with some perspective. The faith journey has been a struggle for me, for being in the Christian ministry has not made it easy to own up to doubt.

What actually happens when faith grows, or does not grow? Is faith "natural" for everyone, part of the process of maturing, or is faith participation in the "miraculous," changing a person's growth in a startling way? Growth in faith is a fascinating subject! Every person, whether they acknowledge it or not, responds to life either with faith or without it. They are trying to make sense of their lives.

CHAPTER ONE

Faith Grows

In considering the faith journey, is it important to understand what is meant by "growth in faith"? Everyone will define this differently, but for the author, growth in faith is a spiritual development, a continuously widening response to stimulation of the person's spirit. This growth in awareness of things spiritual develops an *openness to life*. It is difficult to talk about faith as openness without specifying: Openness to what? This again is personal, but for the author, faith is defined as finding meaning in life. Obviously it is hard to talk about this without referring to ultimate meaning, God. In this book, though, we will try to confine ourselves to discussing faith as the person's *response* to the faith object, or to God. This response changes over the years, and so we can talk about these changes as being growth, or conversely, that which negates growth.

It is not easy to agree on a definition for faith, but we need one! It is important to be clear on this. For some people faith is a value system which they adhere to, like democracy or the doctrine of a certain religious denomination, but this is a narrow definition of faith.

Faith in this book is defined as that which gives meaning to life; it is a way of looking at all of life. A person may have faith in a "faith object", such as God or Allah, in a person, or even in his or her roots. A person could also place faith in parental heritage, the worth ethic, money, Buddha, or in certain values that give life meaning, such as family ties or honesty. These are faith objects.

There are actually two parts to the definition of faith: one a

13

noun, the other a verb. Faith as noun is the faith object: God, or Allah, or material success, or whatever goal that a person is reaching for. The other part of the faith definition views faith as a verb: it is the person's response to the faith object. This faith response some call "faithing." It is "faithing," as a person's response to the faith object, that actually changes and grows. These changes can be noted, and will ultimately affect a person's perspective of the faith object. So the object of faith, whether it be God or some other, changes in the person's perception. This is often confusing to the beholder; faith then is shaken and doubt enters.

This book will try to trace the faithing responses, or the person's "faithing." A spiral model is used to describe some of the faithing responses through life. Spirals are helpful because they are a flexible model for organizing these responses. A ladder or road as a model for the faith journey would be too fixed on goals; faith is more than the process to a goal. Each spiral in the Spiral Faith Model represents clusters of experiences and choices in the various phases of life. A particular spiral represents the phase in life of greatest openness to a particular gift, though this in no way limits gifts to just those indicated. Faith is multidirectional and is as complicated as each individual life.

The faith journey is part of human development through the life cycle. We are indebted to stage theorists for showing us that life, even adult life, moves along in sequence from stage to stage.

(For more on Stage Theory please refer to the Appendix.) There is nothing static about human beings, we are changing constantly, learning constantly, whether age 12 or 80. This built-in human tendency toward development has long been recognized by parents and professionals in childhood education, but only recently by adults and those promoting adult learning.

Can we talk about faith in terms of human development? Can changes in faithing be called "developmental"? One thing is certain, faith does grow and change, it is developmental, but its growth direction is towards that which is transcendent rather than towards becoming better and better. The direction for change in faith is not always upward or towards strengthening and wholeness. Growth in faith often seems to move three steps forward and two backwards! Moreover, the person when considering his or her faith may be struck by an uneasy feeling that "little of this is real." After all, trying to make meaning out of one's life questions the reality of everything. There may be a vague feeling of "something missing." Sadly, by the end of their lives some people may feel bitter, feeling a sense of loss because they never found what they were looking for.

So, patterns for growth in faith *and* retreat from faith are observable in the faith journey. What this book hopes to do is identify the faith responses in various spirals, with each spiral representing a certain cluster of opportunities. Each spiral is fashioned by maturation, experience, and previous opportunities. These are the periods in our lives of greatest openness. Understanding them gives hope, even though there is often discouragement along the faith journey. Spirals invite the person to face with hope what life offers, both positive and negative, and to journey toward those opportunities as unique individuals.

CHAPTER TWO

The Spiral Faith Model

In my mind's eye, life has many spirals circling 'round. I am moving on this spiral. Spirals keep circling in and out, up and down, always in motion. There doesn't seem to be a fixed order, but a certain spiral does seem to dominate for a moment (or years) then moves on to make way for another. Some spirals swoop free while others are tense and awkward.

Spirals speak to me of life and of growth in faith in a balanced way. A three-dimensional spiral model would show the need for a balance in each spiral, a balance between the negative and positive tensions in life. So it is with the various faith tasks facing each person: balance brings wholeness. It is not necessarily tension that is the problem, but lack of wholeness. A lack of balance will bring pain.

Such a model offers an interesting framework for faith development, reminding us that growth in faith is cyclic, ever expanding, not cast in stone. There is also a distinctive emphasis in each spiral, repeating itself at ever more challenging levels, yet maintaining a flexible whole. Spirals as a model for the faith journey remind the reader that life is an exciting challenge with a multidirectional focus. There are ups and downs!

As with most models, the spiral model suffers the usual perception problems. One person doesn't always see the same thing as another person. Yet, I still think that this is an intriguing model for growth in faith. What is faith like — what are its parts? I hope that the Spiral Faith Model will help to throw light on each person's faith experience.

In this model for faith development the following assumptions are made:

1) Faith is the network that gives life its shape and meaning.

2) Faithing is the person's response to life's opportunities, which come as gifts.

3) The person's task is to incorporate these faith gifts into life.

4) Faith is strengthened through openness to life and the appropriation of gifts.

5) The response to gifting is indicative of growth in faith, while a lack of response indicates the negation of faith.

6) Openness to receiving faith gifts depends on the achieving of psycho-social balance in previous spirals.

7) The overall direction for growth in faith is beyond self-actualization towards self-transcendency.

8) Transitions are the time of greatest growth in faith, moving the person from within self to beyond self.

In the Spiral Faith Model, the tie that draws the spirals together is the faith nourishment line flowing through the spirals. This line represents the receiving of and the appropriation of faith gifts throughout life, or conversely, the rejection of and inability to appropriate faith. The faith gifts noted in each spiral are the dominant gift of a cluster of many gifts. It is not intended to limit gifts in any way. These gifts help the person reach for fulfillment throughout the life cycle from birth to death, and beyond. Such faith gifts as trust, joy, a sense of worth, and love are gifts in the sense that they are achieved through openness, they can only be received, not controlled. Such gifts are the gifts of grace.

Within the faith journey there is a special reality — that life is a gift. Recognition of this reality gives meaning to each individual life. "Faith is the container for life," is the way one friend reacted to the model. Spirals do offer a pattern for viewing life as a whole, but the term "container" tends to limit perception of the scope of faith gifts. Faith gifts do not constrict life, they support and expand it giving life its shape and fulfillment.

The following outline of the Spiral Faith Model (See Figure 2) is described in detail in subsequent chapters, and forms the framework for my own faith story found in Chapters 6 to 9. Including some details from my own personal faith story is not intended to suggest that I know the way, or walk in it! There have been many struggles and life has not always been seen as gifted. It is hoped, however, that the inclusion of the faith story will stimulate others to bring into focus their own faith story and so learn to appreciate their own growth spiral.

Stages 1–6: SELF-ACTUALIZATION

1. INCARNATING.
"Ahh. . ." (Birth to circa 6 months) Embedded in the family. Psychosocial task: basic trust/mistrust.
FAITH GIFT: TRUST This is Simple Faith.

2. EXPLORING. "Yes ! Yes! No! No!" (Circa 6 months to 2 years) Embedded in feelings. Psychosocial task: autonomy/shame, doubt.
FAITH GIFT: JOY. This is Initiative Faith.

3. SELFING. "That's mine!" (Circa 2 to 5 years) Embedded in needs.
Psychosocial task: initiative/guilt. FAITH GIFT: O.K.NESS. This is Literal Faith.

4. SCHOOLING. "Can I?" (Circa 6 to 11 years) Embedded in skills.
Psychosocial task: industry/inferiority. FAITH GIFT: LIFE STORIES. This is Learned Faith.

5. INTER-PERSONAL. "Why should I!" (Circa 12 to 14 years) Embedded in the peer group. Psychosocial task: affiliation/abandonment
FAITH GIFT: FORGIVENESS.
This is Relational Faith.

6. INTRA-INDIVIDUAL. "Why did I?" (Circa 15 to 21 years) Embedded in cultural systems.
Psychosocial task: identity/identity confusion. SELF-OTHER TRANSITION FAITH GIFT: ACCEPTANCE OF DIFFERENCE. This is Searching Faith.

Stages 7–12: SELF-TRANSCENDENCE

7. INTRO-VOCATIONAL. "Show me how." (circa 22 to 29 years) Embedded in discipleship (roles) Psychosocial task: intimacy/isolation.
FAITH GIFT: LOVE. This is Reflective Faith.

8. INTRO-WORLD. "I care." (Circa 30 to 39 years). Embedded in stewardship.
Psychosocial task: generativity/stagnation.
FAITH GIFT: CARING. This is Serving Faith.

9. EXTRA-SELF. "It's too much!" (Circa 40 to 55 years) Embedded in experience Psychosocial task: integrity/despair.
OTHER-WITHIN TRANSITION
FAITH GIFT: ACCEPTANCE OF LIMITS. This is Suffering Faith.

10. SPIRITUAL "Hanging loose". (Circa 55 to 65 years) Embedded in perspective Psychosocial task: interiorizing/separating FAITH GIFT: LETTING GO. This is Liberating Faith.

11. TRANSITIONAL. "Now what?" (Circa 65 to 75 years) Embedded in change Psychosocial Task: expanding/constricting
WITHIN-BEYOND TRANSITION
FAITH GIFT: HOPE. This is Renewing Faith.

12. TRANSCENDING. "My life is held." (Circa 75 plus years) Embedded in faith.
Psychosocial Task: trust/fear FAITH GIFT: PEACE. This is Resurrection Faith.

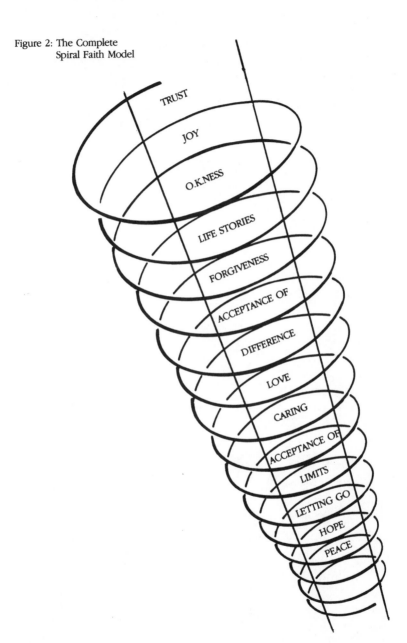

Figure 2: The Complete
Spiral Faith Model

TRUST

JOY

O.K.NESS

LIFE STORIES

FORGIVENESS

ACCEPTANCE OF

DIFFERENCE

LOVE

CARING

ACCEPTANCE OF

LIMITS

LETTING GO

HOPE

PEACE

CHAPTER THREE

Childhood Spirals:

Twelve Spirals in Faith Growth

INCARNATING (Birth to circa six months) "Ahh . . ."

The use of the term "incarnating," as in the incarnation of Jesus,
may startle some people, but here it refers to the human spirit
made flesh at birth. Life itself is a gift, a gift of the spirit, literally.
It should be noted that all age references in this model are in
brackets, as a spiral is not limited to a certain age period. The
model does indicate, however, that a person's openness to specific faith gifts and the balancing of certain psychosocial tasks
are more likely to occur during the spiral indicated.

Newborn babies can at first see very little, but as the imme-
diate environment unfolds, they are looking everywhere, fascinated. Eventually, they will reach out a hand for something to
grasp. Everyone delights in looking at a baby, the focus of all
those gazing eyes, and so baby experiences embeddedment in
the family. All those eyes seem to say, "Hi!" We used to have a
mothers' group in the church where women brought their
babies and kept them on the rug at their feet. Most of the time
everything went fine but when the group bowed heads to pray,
the babies cried! Does baby feel left out because mummy shuts
her eyes? The group solved the problem by praying with open
eyes. Growing trust is a function of inclusion: "I feel safe and
wanted here."

Referring to psychologist Erik Erikson's first "stage task" of trust/mistrust, we note the baby experiences trust as the parents feed, cuddle, and change diapers. Unfortunately, it is impossible to just experience trust and never know mistrust, even in a loving family. Nothing is as secure and beneficial as the womb. Birth is traumatic and can possibly even be experienced as rejection! When baby is laid immediately on mother's tummy, the trauma is reduced.

It is the balance between basic trust and mistrust that affects all subsequent growth. When a person has achieved a degree of resolution between both, tension is reduced and there is openness to reaching out, to growth. This openness affects growth in faith. If the infant fails to incorporate trust at this early age, which is such a basic gift for life, there will be trouble later. Such a person will have trouble trusting God, or self, or others.

In this first spiral, Simple Faith is experienced through intuition, at the feeling level. Years later, if trust as a gift has not been realized, a person may try praying, "Oh God, help me to be more trusting," but won't feel more trusting. There is always the possibility, though, for trust to grow in any subsequent spiral if the person can reach out and experience trust in a relationship. Unfortunately, people are not as readily open to the gift of trust later in their lives as they were in their first few months of life.

2) EXPLORING (Circa age six months to two years) "Yes! Yes! No! No!"

The growing infant experiences the world by feel, intuitively. Smiles and frowns are imitated impulsively, as parents and baby outdo each other smiling. The growing toddler's usual reaction to everything is either "yes," or "no," based on feelings. Baby is reaching into cupboards, placing everything into the mouth, with delight, learning by feel! A child of this age also likes to control and manipulate things. Try playing ball with a toddler and she will hold on to it. When she does throw it and mummy throws it back, what joy! A smile breaks all over her face. In later years if a person hesitates before starting something new, it would be appropriate to wonder what happened to one's delight in exploring. Did it get put down for reaching into too many kitchen cupboards during this spiral?

The intuitive side of faith is therefore experienced as a passion, a joy! The faith gift of joy allows a person to laugh, and laughter will lighten the weight of care. If a child is not allowed to be curious and learn what to poke into and what to leave alone, she will not achieve a balance, in Erikson's language, between autonomy and shame. Having had one's fingers slapped too often, a person will be filled with shame: there will be no joy in reaching out. It is very important for parents to discipline in such a way that a growing toddler develops in autonomy and can appropriate the joy that he or she experiences from exploring new things. Faith is delighting in life, in exploring and appreciating the world. It will be difficult to grow in faith in subsequent years if the child or adult does not feel secure in reaching out.

In this spiral, faith is experienced through imitation as a toddler follows what Mummy and Daddy do, reaching out with the same look and mannerisms. Faith in this sense is Imitative Faith.

3) SELFING (Circa age two to five years) "That's mine!"

At first, children of this age are not going to be able to tell the difference between what is theirs and what is yours. "What's mine is mine, and what's yours is mine!" There is nothing more bossy than a five-year-old at play. The preschooler is embedded in needs and wishes and goes after them until hearing the reprimand from parents and others, "Share that toy with your brother!" Then there is guilt.

Initiative can be weakened by guilt. Too much guilt sets up an internal struggle that immobilizes action. The balance between Erikson's initiative and guilt greatly affects growth in faith, for it affects reaching out. Children who do not know how to relate to other children without guilt are stymied at play. They need to know self as O.K., and when told something they did is O.K., accept it without question. An adult friend once said, "My parents told everybody but me that I was a great little kid. I wish they had told me."

In this spiral, faith is literal. The preschooler doesn't question parental words or actions. Adults can get into difficult situations thinking there is a lot of explaining to do only to find the child takes the explanation literally. A friend told of what happened when a neighbour died recently. Granny was trying to explain death to her four-year-old grandchild. When asked what had happened to the man next door Granny said, "He has gone up to heaven to live among the stars." As Granny was wondering how to explain further the little girl replied, "Oh, can we look up there tonight and see him?" This is Literal Faith. The adult who remains in this early faith spiral will see the devil with horns and heaven paved with gold.

4) SCHOOLING (Circa age six to eleven) "Can I?"

In school the child learns various skills, and is helped to recognize his or her abilities. According to Erikson, the psychosocial task here is to adjust to the tension between industry and inferiority. What are the skills a child has in comparison with skills others have? Does the child feel inferior? Through doing, hearing, and seeing what others are up to, the school-age child learns the skills necessary to relate. A child can be happily industrious, doing something well, knowing that he or she is not too different, or conversely, unhappy, not wanting to try, feeling she or he is inferior. A child who is having difficulty balancing between industry and inferiority will constantly ask "Can I?" before doing anything.

The school-age child loves to listen to stories, identifying with the good characters and playing along with the bad. The lives of other people are gift to the child who listens to Granddad's stories. Learning the skill of reading opens the child to the world of others. In listening to fairy tales, hero stories or Bible stories, the child in spiral 4 is fascinated. Children learn about life itself from story-telling, but in this spiral there is no reflection on the story's effect or meaning.

At this stage, faith is experienced as something learned from others — it is a Learned Faith. In school the child is taking in facts and situations, assimilating beliefs and value as seen through the lives of others. There is little awareness of personal implications. Many adults remain in this faith spiral all their lives, listening to the Gospel without integrating the truths expressed there into their own lives.

5) INTER-PERSONAL (Circa age twelve to fourteen) "Why should I?"

The teenager is embedded in the peer group, as friends now have a greater influence than family. Friendship means that things are done together, with mutual interests. Family members are not looked on as friends, they are just family, and the home is often just a place to sleep. Mutuality, or solidarity, with the peer group is very important in this spiral. When asked, "Where are you going?" the teen is likely to respond, "Oh, just around," meaning out with friends and anywhere but home. The psychosocial task here, affiliation/abandonment, is discussed in Robert Kegan's book, *The Responsible Self*.[1] Kegan has incorporated the concept of growth through relationship in his model, though the age range considered here is not necessarily the same as Kegan's.

There is nothing more lonely than a teenager without friends. This is the beginning of a major social problem, that of the loneliness and the sensation of abandonment. What is needed is a Relational Faith, where one can personally relate to the faith object as friend. Jesus as a friend can be a meaningful concept in this spiral.

The teenager can easily feel as if he or she has made a mess of things and needs at least one good friend to ease the agony of rejection by peers. Friends can get angry, and so for a friendship to last, it must experience those times when forgiveness is shared with "I'm sorry!" In this relationship the gift of forgiveness is important if a person is going to grow in faith and reach out to others. Just saying, "I'm sorry", though, is not enough. Forgiveness flows both ways — it is a gift exchanged in relationship. Forgiveness is returned as acceptance by a parent, a friend, a teacher, a coach, or a minister. Then a teenager knows what affiliation really is: it is forgiveness in action. It is important in this spiral to experience faith through relationship and so be able to experience a relationship with God through forgiveness. The faith gift of forgiveness is basically acceptance of self. It's very hard to forgive someone when one can't forgive oneself.

6) INTRA-INDIVIDUAL (Circa fifteen to twenty-one) "Why did I?"

This spiral may include young teens and young adults leaving home to go to college, or live in an apartment, or even live on the street. An early transition out of the home is more frequent in our society, with its emphasis on autonomy instead of relationship. It is a time when the young person discovers that he or she is embedded in all kinds of systems. Along with the family, school, gang, and church, there is college, the first job, marriage, first home and mortgage, perhaps even a first child. This is a very important transition time during which a young adult can feel very restless, as if all of life is up for grabs. It is the transition from SELF TO OTHERS, and sometimes self feels as if it is being squeezed out while trying to fit in with others.

Using Erikson's identity/identity confusion task, we can see that confusion arises during a crisis about self. It is important to establish who one is in relation to these systems. A person can get lost in this spiral, trying out different things. Young people need space to search and question as they try to find themselves. Churches should have room in their expectations for young people with a Searching Faith. They need to find themselves without having to adhere to a rigid doctrine and fixed (read boring) practices. This is especially true in our multicultural society with its varied values and expectations. Yet these very differences come as gifts to a person seeking to be a part of it all. They widen the person's horizons.

In this spiral, the faith gift of "acceptance of difference" is incorporated into a person's life as he or she tries to appreciate and value these differences and find acceptance within them. When young adults do not find acceptance, or a place to be oneself, they will struggle at length through this mid-twenty transition of SELF TO OTHER and turn back on SELF. This transition is very important for faith as it is the move to own oneself, to discover one's identity. Only then can a person reach out to others with confidence. Women can have trouble with this transition if their identity has been shaped by overdependence on family members or husband. Men can have trouble with this transition if their identity has been shaped by independence from family members or peers (i.e., too much autonomy).

This spiral involves a search for truth, truth about self and one's world. In this search one can get very grumpy, feeling as if the self is a mess. This Searching Faith is looking for personal meaning. When there is a struggle with self with a poor identity formation, there will be trouble accepting and being part of a belief system. The person will be unable to commit himself to anything, not to another person, not even to God. She will not feel secure enough to reach out. Such a person will find it is impossible to grow in faith beyond this spiral until this identity confusion is settled. Some adults never move beyond this spiral.

The SELF TO OTHER transition is vital to faith as it is a decisive move towards self-transcendence, moving beyond oneself. If faith is to grow, it must be able to search for truth: to own self as an integral part of life. Owning one's identity forms the base from which a person reaches out with confidence to others. Unfolding personal truth during the SELF TO OTHER transition becomes the crux of one's inner core. This is a major faith transition. As the person moves through this spiral by achieving a measure of self-actualization, he or she starts to move towards self-transcendence.

Footnotes

[1]Robert Kegan, *The Evolving Self: Problem and Process in Human Development* (Cambridge: Harvard University Press, 1982).

CHAPTER FOUR

Adult Spirals

7) INTRO-VOCATIONAL (Circa age twenty-two to twenty-nine) "Show me how."

The young adult continues to learn the tasks and skills needed for life, especially for the chosen career. It is a period of apprenticeship, or discipleship, learning from a mentor. In this spiral, Erikson's psychosocial task is to balance the tension between intimacy and isolation. How far one should go in intimate relationships is of primary concern. What is privacy? What is intimacy? Falling in love, marrying, and having close relationships all reflect whether a person has adjusted the tension between intimacy and isolation. Some men in this spiral can have trouble with intimacy if they have developed a strong identity based on autonomy, or separation from others. Men are often forced in our society to "stand on their own feet." This makes it difficult to forge interdependence in relationships.

It is the young adult's commitment to the mentor, the loved one, the boss, that influences growth. Learning is primarily through a relationship with that mentor. Growth in faith in this spiral comes through commitment to learn about the goals and values of the mentor. This can include commitment to Jesus or to some other highly-valued mentor.

Through close relationships, a person grows in faith by moving toward self-transcendency, giving self to another in love. A person must be free to choose to appropriate the gift of love into their lives or be free to reject it. This choice is influenced by the psychosocial adjustment to intimacy and isolation. Lacking an integration of love within self, a person will struggle in isolation, remaining fearful of opening up to others. Such people are not able to love themselves and therefore find it difficult to love another.

As is true of all faith gifts, love can be available throughout life — it is not limited to this spiral. But the person is most open to love in this spiral. Love comes as a gift through the loving acceptance of other people. However, the ability to love oneself is a result of reflection: "I am loved, I am O.K." This ability to love oneself, to appreciate oneself, is basic for faith to reach beyond self. When a person does not appreciate and accept self, it is almost impossible to love others, or to accept the love of God as real.

An integration of love and the self is possible within an understanding of how love affects relationships. This awareness comes with the Reflective Faith that helps develop understanding. Such understanding grows through the longing to be open to love in this spiral. Young adults spend many a night feeling, wondering, thinking, praying. But this reflection is not necessarily an analysis of the self, or pulling self apart. We can ask, "What is the use in what I do?" A Reflective Faith involves understanding and accepting both strengths and weaknesses, and deciding on a course of action.

A Reflective Faith also knows that love must be given freely or it is manipulation; love is not lust. Growth in faith frees a person from trying to manipulate another to fill personal needs, and from using the other person. Freely reaching out in love is growth towards self-transcendency, for love shared moves a person beyond his or her own needs to concern for the needs of the loved one. This seventh spiral is a major growth experience for faith, as the person, becoming aware of the cost to self, still loves.

Putting love into action is life's vocation; it is the call to be fully alive through loving relationships. A good resolution of the challenges in this spiral results in high motivation and satisfaction. We see this when a love for the job makes the work place a creative place. Such people see their work as part of a larger reality and feel "it was all worthwhile."

8) INTRO-WORLD (Circa age thirty to thirty-nine) "I care."

This is a very active and busy time in a person's life, with more
and more responsibilities demanding attention. A person may
be promoted into a more demanding managerial position at
work, and the children may need more attention at home. Caring a lot, most people put their shoulder to the wheel and push.
They hope to change things and make this world a better place
for their children. In this spiral a person is embedded in the
stewardship of this world's goods. "I have so much! I am a care-
giver, literally, and I feel guilty about saying No!" Following
Erikson's stages, a person is now trying to balance generativity
and stagnation. "Generativity" is trying to make this world a better place for others. Conversely, stagnating is not caring at all,
and doing nothing.

The tension between doing and being during this spiral is
difficult to keep in balance. Many people feel guilty just taking a
holiday, and are much happier when they are working. Weari-
ness and inability to resolve the problems one sees all around
can lead to apathy and stagnation. Or, there is the possibility of
becoming overstimulated and caring too much, which leads to
being drained. The result is often depression. Such a person
feels, "It doesn't matter what I do, nothing will change anyway."
In the midst of this tension the gift of caring for another person
is experienced as affirmation. The more a person can participate in this kind of caring, the more there is opportunity for personal fulfillment through serving others. This is a Serving Faith.
People believe in what they do and willingly lend a helping
hand. Such a caring attitude is the result of a continuous moving away from what self wants to what others need, towards self-
transcendency. Because people are very busy in this spiral there
is little time for reflection and little time for church. Faith is now
putting love into action

9) EXTRA-SELF (Circa age forty to fifty-five) "It's too much!"

As the years go by, the caring adult continues to feel that there is
so much pain and deprivation in the world. Who can do any-

thing about the threat of nuclear war or unemployment. One's own life holds the possibility of developing cancer or AIDS. What good has it all been? In questioning the meaning of one's actions, faith will be tested. The struggle here is basically with one's attitude to what one can accomplish, not with life itself.

Integrity, or looking at one's life and owning it, means that a person must be honest with self, without pretense. This is Erikson's psychosocial task in this spiral. Integrity is acknowledging that "I would not change any of my life even if it were possible." Despair is the denial of self-worth, feeling that "I would change most of it if I could, but I can't. It seems like everything I did was a failure." There are so many limits now to what a person finds he or she can do. Physical limits start to appear; perhaps even playing in a ball game is too much. Emotional limits, health limits, and many other limits force people to accept that they are not superwoman, or superman, and they are never going to be! The faith gift here is the personal graciousness to accept limits and the finding of other ways to express the self's worth.

Some people in their forties don't want to accept these limits and turn their lives upside-down looking for a new start with a job, or with a new spouse, or a new house. It has become fashionable to look at this as the "mid-life crisis." Unfortunately, we can't turn ourselves in for a refit, as if life just needed a new set of clothes. Many go back to college, or take counselling to help develop a new attitude to self, a more accepting, realistic attitude. The Spiral Faith Model calls this transition the move from other to within, from caring to integrating mind and body. The changes in this spiral are often acknowledged in the middle of suffering, an inner suffering. A restlessness descends that can only be described as pain with one's lot. It is an inner pain that encourages a journey within self to ease the pain and accept the limits. This sets the person free to move out again.

This spiral allows the person to move through a transcendent crisis, beyond personal limits to a non-physical reality within, a spiritual reality. A balance here is achieved when a person can "centre down" within, interiorizing one's worth. Then a person's life can be acknowledged as a worthwhile part of a larger whole. Here, no one has to push to prove that he or she is worthy of a place in the universe. One accepts that life is a gift, and is O.K. as it is.

When a severely handicapped person plays piano from a wheelchair and leads the singing at a conference, it never ceases to inspire others. When such people tell their story, they are obviously fully alive, having moved through this transition and accepted themselves. They inspire others because they have risen above limits; in telling their story, their spirit soars. This experience of freedom from limits is basic in the journey towards transcendency. Suffering is often the door through which a person must pass to accept limits. This is a Suffering Faith that, in Christian terms, is a crucifixion. It leads to personal resurrection.

10) SPIRITUAL (Circa age fifty-five to sixty-five) "Hanging loose."

As a person moves through the OTHER TO WITHIN transition, there is more awareness of one's inner, spiritual world. This inner life has a freedom about it that allows a person to be released from worrying about "what other people think." Being at last adjusted to personal limits and having found other ways to do things, such persons are free to be themselves. They can be serious or ridiculous, no matter which, for their personal qualities are now based on integrity.

Unfortunately, as they approach retirement, many people become bitter and disillusioned. Not having moved through the last transition successfully, they are still suffering. Such people may also be tied down by circumstances beyond their control, which feeds negative attitudes. The psychosocial task here, interiority in balance with separation, can only be achieved when a person has moved through the OTHERS TO WITHIN transition. If this centering down within has not been achieved, people will withdraw into themselves while cutting other people out.

There is tremendous conflict here within the self, between owning the truth about self and caring about what others think of you. One's personal self-image can be badly damaged forcing one to hold on desperately. More than ever, there is the challenge to experience steadiness within in order to reach out. Sadly, many continue to hold on tightly and withdraw. They separate themselves from other people and stay home more and more. There is much loneliness. The psychosocial task of interiorizing/separating is not in balance. The person has separated from self.

But into every negative situation can come the faith gift of letting go. Several years ago a friend was leaving in a hurry to fly home to Ireland as her mother was dying. As she got on the plane someone told her to remember that when the going got tough to, "Let go and let God." She didn't have a clue how to do that, having trouble letting go at any time! Then one night, as she lay awake worrying about her mother, she felt she just couldn't take any more, and started shaking. Was she going to go to pieces and be no good to anyone? In her despair this was the prayer that escaped from her lips, "Oh God, I can't go on. You take over from here." Then she knew that she had "let go and let God," and was at peace. This is Liberating Faith, experiencing the freedom of being fully oneself even in weakness. Such growth in faith moves a person to be released from the self's worries, and be strengthened within.

11) TRANSITIONAL (Circa sixty-five to seventy-five) "Now what?"

"Now what?" reflects a life that is embedded in so much change, the person almost seems afloat. Retirement brings on the mid-sixty transition, a period of adjustment with many major changes. The story is told about a man we will call Tom. When Tom turned sixty-five, he had to retire from his job at the waterworks department. The hardest thing he remembers having to do was to turn in his keys. He had a large ring of keys, one to every room at the plant. After he turned them in he felt like an outsider, no longer wanted or needed. After retirement a person is quickly replaced. This means a major adjustment, especially if the person sees his worth only in his work, and not in himself as an individual.

Retirement can also introduce major adjustments with fi-
nances. If one can afford it, there may be an opportunity for
travel, or at least time now to do all those things that were just
dreams before. Unfortunately, the reality is often vastly different
from the dream. What can one hope for now? This situation
makes the faith gift of renewal of hope imperative. There is
nothing left for some but memories. Older people are great story-tellers! Reminiscing lets a person look over her life and accept
it as it has been. In another's appreciation there is hope to be
found, hope of some worth to someone.

Without a sense of hope some people in this spiral may close
down on the self and narrow their horizons, becoming very quiet and withdrawn. They are having trouble balancing the
psychosocial task of expanding /constricting. The faith gift of
hope allows a person to continue expanding life's experiences.
This faith gift is not just a hoping for things to be different. Rather, it is the gift of hope in that which is larger than self, to participate in that which is more than the present moment. In this spiral, where one's life is often constricted physically, hope is realized if the person has been able to transcend limits in spiral 10
and reach out for that which is transcendent, beyond self. This
mid-sixty transition involves a major faith growth movement
from WITHIN TO BEYOND.

In the developed industrialized nations, projections of future
increases in an aging population make it imperative that the life
and worth of those over sixty-five be affirmed. This is a Renewing Faith, as people find new and ever-expanding ways to affirm
life and offer their talents in the service of others. Some even
travel overseas, offering their business skills to undeveloped
countries. The WITHIN TO BEYOND transition is transcendent
in that skills are not necessarily appreciated for their monetary
value, but for a deeper value. As it moves a person from WITH-
IN TO BEYOND, this transition prepares that person for life beyond the physical self, for finding life's supreme meaning and
fulfillment in the spirit. This is the transition that prepares human beings for the Universal Stage, stage 6 in James Fowler's
model.

12) TRANSCENDING (Circa age seventy-five, plus) "My life is held."

In this spiral, "My life is held" reflects the deep trust of a person whose life is embedded in faith. (Compare the first spiral.) A person by now has appropriated many of the faith gifts and has come to experience life as held together by faith. Faith is the framework that for years has given encouragement for growth. Faith's development has been balanced between physical and spiritual needs, and social and psychological factors. In other words, it is a holistic faith. Many will say here that this is too idealistic, that few people are this well-balanced. But faith by its very nature surrounds life with hope. Change and growth are possible at every age.

In this final spiral, a person has a tremendous ability to enjoy little things which to others would seem insignificant, but to the older person are precious. "Long ago" things seem clearer now and are greatly valued. To be able to tell others about one's life is an indication of the acceptance of that life, and to live with appreciation of the past. This kind of acceptance also indicates hope for a future and trust in the present. To accept and delight in one's life in this way is to demonstrate a faith-filled life.

When everything eventually has to be done for an elderly person, even feeding and dressing, personal need reflects back to the first spiral and the gift of trust. With physical defences down, the person is vulnerable to the unsolved tensions between life's psychosocial tasks. Or again, it is beautiful to see how openness to faith gifts along the way has moulded character. Trust now steadies the person in the face of mortal fear. There is a balance reached between the psychosocial tasks of trust and fear. The faith gift of peace within transforms a weakened life into a gracious receiver. Such a person knows trust intimately and can openly receive even death.

All of life's faith gifts have strengthened the senior person's ability to be open to receiving and giving. A faithfilled life knows release from fear, for there is already a trust in that which is known, and a hope in that which is not yet known. Here is a person who throughout life has constantly reached out beyond limits and found peace. This is the faith journey almost completed, it is Transcendent Faith, it is a Resurrection Faith, as a person grows beyond self, even beyond death.

Figure 3: Transitions in the
         Spiral Faith Model

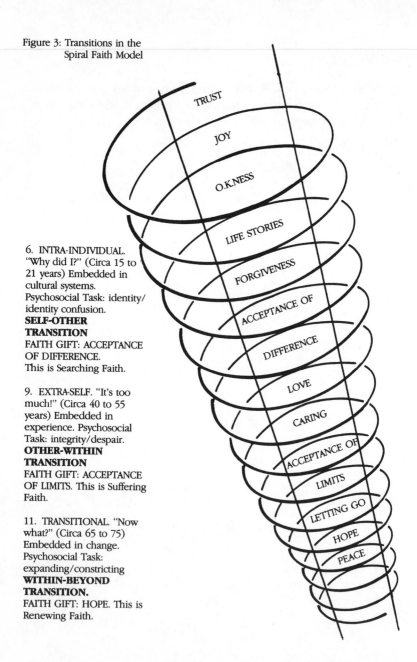

6. INTRA-INDIVIDUAL.
"Why did I?" (Circa 15 to
21 years) Embedded in
cultural systems.
Psychosocial Task: identity/
identity confusion.
SELF-OTHER
TRANSITION
FAITH GIFT: ACCEPTANCE
OF DIFFERENCE.
This is Searching Faith.

9. EXTRA-SELF. "It's too
much!" (Circa 40 to 55
years) Embedded in
experience. Psychosocial
Task: integrity/despair.
OTHER-WITHIN
TRANSITION
FAITH GIFT: ACCEPTANCE
OF LIMITS. This is Suffering
Faith.

11. TRANSITIONAL. "Now
what?" (Circa 65 to 75)
Embedded in change.
Psychosocial Task:
expanding/constricting
WITHIN-BEYOND
TRANSITION.
FAITH GIFT: HOPE. This is
Renewing Faith.

TRUST

JOY

O.K.NESS

LIFE STORIES

FORGIVENESS

ACCEPTANCE OF

DIFFERENCE

LOVE

CARING

ACCEPTANCE OF

LIMITS

LETTING GO

HOPE

PEACE

CHAPTER FIVE

Transitions

There are times in a person's life when faith grows in leaps and bounds. What generates such growth? Can these leaps be identified and explained? The concept of "transitions" in development theory offers some interesting thoughts in this regard. There are periods in life when a person struggles against conflicting circumstances and personal crises. Such periods are called developmental transitions and they have a lasting effect on a person's faith.

When considering the ongoing faith journey, it is of interest to note that a person seems to be more open to receiving faith gifts in transition times. If we were to chart our faith journey, we would probably notice the peaks and valleys. These would most likely occur in the search for meaning during transition times, as a person struggles to make changes. Transitions are risky seasons of change. As a person looks for help and the strength to "get through," they tend to be more open. It is no accident that most religious faith expressions are about courage in times of trial, in other words, during transitions.

Daniel Levinson's book, *The Seasons of a Man's Life*,[1] introduced readers to a pattern with transitions among the seasons in a person's life. Others have documented the various developmental tasks which apply to each transition. Levinson's book has directed our attention to the times in our lives of greatest struggle. When these struggles are positively resolved, it is a season of great potential for growth.

Some think Levinson's research is flawed in that it refers just to men, while some readers make the assumption that his seasons apply to all adults. But women do go through similar transitions, though the content and timing are different. For both men and women, transitions force a person to question and search, opening them to faith. A study of faith choices made in the various transitions of life would probably show a great deal about how faith grows, or the reverse, how faith is diminished.

In his book, Levinson refers to five adult transitions.

First: During the late teens and early twenties, there is the move away from the family home and settling down on one's own. There is the first job, the first love, and perhaps marriage.

Second: At age thirty there is the move to the second home, and perhaps into the managerial position. There may be a struggle to find one's place, to make a good living, and get to the top.

Third: In the forties a person faces the mid-life crisis or the waking up to life as "the same old thing without its glow." There is much restlessness, wondering what else life has to offer.

Fourth: Physical changes through the fifties force one to accept change. Adjustments are needed when the body just won't do what it used to, especially in physical sports.

Fifth: There is the late-adult transition into retirement with its enforced lay-offs, bringing with it changes to a person's income and daily schedule.

A transition is a challenging period, as the person leaves behind that which is secure and known and reaches for the unknown. Transitions are a prime time for growth if change is positive and balance is retained. As Vivian McCoy has said in her *Life Cycle Training Manual*, "For growth to occur, challenges need to be slightly greater than the individual's present coping skills so that he/she can stretch, yet not be overwhelmed and forced to retreat to safer ground."[3] For this reason, the person in a transition needs much support or the change will be negative, and growth stunted.

It is obvious that transitions can be vital for growth, especially growth in faith. In each transition, as a person reaches out from

Figure 4: Levinson's Transitions[2]

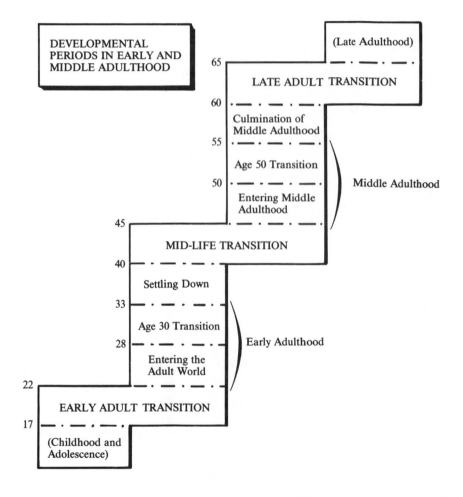

relative security towards what is basically unknown, faith can grow in leaps and bounds, for faith is basically trusting in that which is beyond self. Transition times can then move the person out of self towards self-transcendence. During the major faith transition, the movement is three-fold: out of self towards others; within self for that which represents personal meaning; beyond self to that which is greater than self. For this reason, the Spiral Faith Model identifies three of Levinson's transitions as important for faith and identifies them as follows:

The EARLY ADULT transition is a movement from SELF TO OTHERS.
The MID-FORTY transition is a movement from OTHERS TO WITHIN.
The MID-SIXTY transition is a movement from WITHIN TO BEYOND.

The faith journey is enriched with this movement from self through life to the beyond. During these transitions the person is vulnerable, and more open to finding out truth about self, others, God, and the universe. Transition times then offer the greatest opportunity for growth in transcendence, for growth in faith.

These transition times are usually a struggle, and can last for months and years. There is the struggle to let go of the known. Then after accepting change there is security for a while, only to be replaced by further transition. A person will sometimes seek relief through such bandaid solutions as snuffing cocaine, or using alcohol, or abusing subscription drugs, without realizing that this struggle goes to life's roots and involves self-worth. Not wanting to be aware of the painful self, a person will seek a cover-up, making the journey to finding oneself much harder. Transitions always involve decision-making while the person struggles with the ego. "Do I, or don't I?" Decision-making is often fraught with pain and confusion, especially when former transitions weren't well handled.

Most transitions are full of excitement as well as fear of the unknown. There is the first day at school with its high excite-

ment and fear. Then again in adolescence there is the fear of
not fitting in at Junior High. There is the first year in college, or
at work. There is the marriage, and the new baby. All these transitions can be exciting and scary. They will be painful when previous struggles have not been resolved in earlier transitions. The
subconscious will feel the lack of security and take much longer
to risk change and growth, if ever.

All transitions in life are important points of change. Decisions are made that affect one's whole future, decisions which
are vital in the faith journey. Having noted the major opportunity transitions give for change and growth, or the reverse, pain
and stagnation, we should carefully consider the implications in
these transitions for church fellowship and support. There is
considerable potential during the transitional times in life, but
often people drop out of church, and other groups, because the
pain and confusion is too much. This is unfortunate, and only
closes off the self to others, unless the hurting person can share
pain with others in a supportive, small-group setting.

Those who are concerned about the faith journey should
take every opportunity to strengthen the supportive fellowship
in churches, to enrich the family unit, to help develop a strong
sense of worth in the child and teenager, to support the bonding of friendships in the young adult, to foster understanding of
the pressures in the work place, and to promote wholesome, intimate relationships. When supported, all developmental transitions are a blessing, a season for growth.

Footnotes
[1]Daniel J. Levinson, *The Seasons of a Man's Life* (New York: Alfred Knopf,
1978).
[2]*Ibid.*
[3]V. R. McCoy, C. Ryan, and J. W. Lichtenberg, *The Adult Life Cycle Training
Manual and Reader* (K. S. Lawrence, Adult Life Resource Center, University of
Kansas, 1978).

CHAPTER SIX

Life on an Island

It's fun to hear a story, but to write one's personal story feels strange and scary. People may read it and know me, somewhat! As I look back over my life there are certain years that influenced my faith more than others, and these I'll include with more detail. My hope in offering this faith story is that it will inspire others to write theirs, and so come to understand their own faith journey a little better.

As I am single, female, and involved with the church, those who share these traits will identify with parts of my story. Most who do will be women. Perhaps they too will have felt powerless at times, as I have. Being in the fifties is an interesting age for looking back over life with some perspective and forward with some expectation. I do not feel that I am over the hump yet but am just getting into those really interesting years, years for more growth.

The Spiral Faith Model provides the framework for this story, with a comment after each spiral on the faith gift. This is the gift that the story teller would have been most open to receiving at that particular spiral. Though these individual gifts are suggested as the faith gift in that spiral, it is probably but the dominant one in a cluster.

MY STORY IN SPIRAL 1
Incarnating (Circa birth to six months)

Once upon a time when Mom and Dad were young and living in Windsor, Nova Scotia, my sister and I arrived. There is a two-year difference between us, which explains why I've always had the feeling that I had to catch up with someone! Evidently there was a blizzard, and I was born! When I was four months old the family moved to Bermuda, where Dad became the minister in St. Andrew's Church, Hamilton. Life on an island! It seems like a dream now, growing up on a beautiful, sunny, coral reef. Life was very leisurely.

During the first six months in Bermuda I had a nanny, a family friend who came to Bermuda with my parents to help, as mother was not well. I wonder if she was paid, for we were very poor. A baby boy who came after me died in childbirth, so when my brother was born, he was special. Years later I met this nanny in Windsor, Nova Scotia, a dear old soul who gave me a big hug. Maybe she gave me lots of hugs when I was a baby. At least, I hope she cuddled me a lot because our parents were very reserved with hugs.

Our house was the converted church hall, with lots of big, drafty rooms to play in. There was no central heating and I was sick a lot. The warmest place in winter was either in bed or in front of the fireplace in the living room. Bermuda winters sometimes had temperatures of 48F. In summer, when it was very hot and humid, I remember sleeping under mosquito netting to keep out the bugs.

Our parents had originally come from New Zealand. Dad left as a young man to study in America. Mother saved up her pennies and chased him — seven years later she finally persuaded him to marry her, urged on by a wire from home. A determined woman was mother! Now three years later, she was living on an island, married to a busy minister, far away from New Zealand. Even though we lived right next to the little pink church, I think mother was lonely. She spent her days looking after us children, and the family's energy revolved around Dad's church.

Comment: The Faith Gift in Spiral 1. "Trust"

What is the most obvious gift in infancy, the basic gift that becomes the root structure for growth in faith? Erikson's first stage task, trust/mistrust, is important as the basis for psychological development. Moreover, trust is also the basic faith gift. If I had

grown up not being able to trust myself, it would be very difficult to trust God or any person. I can trust other people up to a
point, especially church-involved types. I have high expectations of other people and get very disappointed when someone
lets me down. I probably received the gift of trust from my parents and nanny.

It takes a real bonding between baby and parents for trust to
form. Unfortunately, it is only too true that a child rarely grows
up experiencing perfect trust, life being what it is. Total trust is
too idealistic. Many things can happen to weaken the baby's developing trust level, even in a loving home. Indeed, after the
womb experience of high security the birth trauma would be
the first experience of mistrust. Perhaps the baby's experience
of birth is a sense of being ejected, or rejected? What is needed
for growth in faith to occur is a balance between trust and mistrust, as Erikson indicated. This healthy tension is basic for the
faith response of openness to reaching out to God, and others.

Basic trust is appropriated through intuition (not cognition),
and indicates that much of faith is on the feeling level. Trust
must be felt in the home atmosphere! Years later an adult might
try to make the cognitive decision to trust someone, but will
find it hard to hang in there and trust on command.

MY STORY IN SPIRAL 2
Exploring (Circa ages six months to two years)

The stubborn gene in our family descended through my brother, not me. (Some friends will question that!) I was a compliant,
shy little toddler who rarely said "No! No!" like most one-year-
olds. I learned to say "Yes," or kept quiet most of the time. People who know me now can't imagine me being shy, but I was
very shy as a child.

I have no distinct memories of those years, except Dad's
home movies. There is a picture of me playing in the church
grounds next door. I was fascinated with a concrete sundial that
stood about three feet high. I can remember trying to climb up
on it as if it were a mountain. There was great danger for us
growing up in a church yard! We were always watched by par-

ents and congregation. I suspect I was told "No" far more than I said it. I wonder how much emotion I choked off because of watching eyes? Rarely did this serious little toddler laugh.

Great things were expected of us kids! We had to behave — people could see us. To this day I am on guard; rarely do I play until I get my "work" done and rarely do I laugh out loud. Most pictures of us were solemn. We were good little kids, and if we weren't, we learned to hide.

Comment: The Faith Gift in Spiral 2. "Joy"

If joy is the faith gift in spiral 2, I may be a deprived child. Like the faith gift of trust, joy would have had to be appropriated at the intuitive, feeling level. A one-year-old will delight in exploring and shriek with joy at finding. I'm sure I did my share of getting into things, and still delight in trying something out for the first time, but I can't imagine me shrieking with joy and getting away with it. Children were to be seen and not heard in our house! Joy for me is getting my work or project done — writing the day's portion of this book — before I can go and do something else for fun. Joy doesn't come bubbling out of me. I wish it did; life would not be so duty-driven.

Often in church circles we are dealing with a negative tilt in Erikson's psychosocial task of balancing autonomy with shame and doubt. There were too many eyes watching. A favourite saying in our house was, "What will people think?" What was often in doubt was my behaviour. I wonder if most well-meaning Christian parents make it hard for a child to grow in joy and develop a sense of joyful autonomy by imposing on them moralistic demands so early? I can't ever remember my parents delighting in me if I could hear it — that would have instilled in me the sin of pride! So I doubt that this gift got much of a foothold in my sense of autonomy. Even now, as a Christian, joy is something I long for and often wonder about.

Can a person, years later, work at appropriating joy into life if spiral 2 discipline negated it? Again, joy is appropriated by intuition. Joy bubbles out naturally, it cannot be sustained by thought processes for long, or appropriated by inner discipline.

Joy always comes as gift from a loved one, or from God, through his spirit within. Joy as gift can reach us in any spiral but coming after spiral 2 it is harder to appropriate, for joy then tends to be more cognitive than intuitive.

MY STORY IN SPIRAL 3
Selfing (Circa age two to five years)

My sense of self was fashioned in reaction to two pressures, my place in the family and my Dad's reputation. As the middle child, I was often told off by my sister, and my brother would take my toys and break them. Mother had to separate everything we used or we fought. We even had separate jam jars on the table. I remember mine was grape, and it's still my favourite jam. Each of us girls had a doll that drank and wet, with a separate set of clothes. My brother was born early in this spiral, so I expect I felt "put out" literally, spending most of my time outside, wishing I could go to school with my sister. I finally was allowed to attend kindergarten at the age of four. I remember standing in line one day, having my finger nails inspected at school. Mine must have been real dirty

My hair is naturally curly and by age five was so bushy that mother could hardly get the comb through the ringlets on the end of each clump. She would sit me at the piano where I could pretend to play while she combed the knots out. At one point, I got lice in this mop and was doused with kerosene. Can you imagine all that thick hair smelling of kerosene? Dad used to call me his curly top, and threatened to turn me upside-down to use for a mop! I hated my hair!

Comment: The Faith Gift in Spiral 3. "O.K.ness"

Was I a mop or a little girl? I wonder what I thought of myself really? Here was this shy little girl who dragged her feet along the ground following mother home. I don't think I felt very good about myself. Looking back, I wish that someone had given me a hug and told me I was O.K., a nice little kid.

The faith gift in this spiral is the gift of O.K.ness, knowing oneself to be special to someone. If so, it was slow coming my way. There was always some implied criticism given to this curly top. "I could do better if I tried." Erikson's psychosocial task here involves achieving a balance between initiative and guilt. I wonder if guilt overrode initiative in my development. I still have to push myself to get started on things, and this poor self-attitude results in my trying too hard. Remember, I was shy. I also was developing very nicely in insecurity. There were too many people watching and I felt like a mop!

The faith we knew in those early years revolved around church and Sunday School. My Dad as the minister was literally the church. What he said was BIG, he was God in a black gown. Before the church people I could never measure up. Unfortunately, with so many expectations to be good, it was hard to feel O.K. very often.

MY STORY IN SPIRAL 4
Schooling (Circa age six to eleven)

My school was the Bermuda High School for Girls, a private girls' school. Dad and Mother felt it was the only place on the island where my sister and I could get enough schooling to eventually go on to college. Our parents saved up for years to send us all to college. Education was very important; we had to study hard and I'm still at it.

When I was six and in Form One, the family went back to New Zealand on a six months' gift vacation to see the grandmothers who were still alive. This trip is so big in my memory that it blots out most of what went before. I met my cousins for the first time and enjoyed playing with them. I was piggyback riding with one of them — when we tumbled and a broken bone in my foot wasn't discovered until we were back in Bermuda. I guess I was still shy and didn't complain. Complaining was a "No-No" in our family! If we were really sick we had to be running a temperature before getting sent to bed! We all caught the measles in New Zealand so mother had enough to worry about. We also saw snow for the first time, lots of it, but Granny wouldn't let us go outside and play. I can still remember being glued to a window looking wistfully out at all the white stuff.

Back again in Bermuda I was a year behind in school, having missed most of Form One. I never did learn to spell! I was still shy and recess was awful. I would stand under a tree wishing for someone to come and play with me. The only time I would come into my own was sports day. I could run like a deer and the Governor usually handed me trophies for the hundred-yard dash and the relay. The rest of the time I was my father's daughter and never able to forget it. The other girls in school would stop telling dirty jokes when I came in as Dad was on the Board of Governors, and I might tell tales. Dad seemed like a big shot but actually we were very poor. I never had nice clothes. I remember with a squirm one outfit mother brought me. It was a light pink wool dress which I hated with a passion, especially after mother made me wear it to a school picnic. I suppose she thought I would look nice but it just made me look silly.

My school years spanned World War II. Bermuda was practically under siege. Ships bringing food products were regularly torpedoed and the whole island was rationed. We used to listen on the radio to voices from enemy subs circling the islands looking for a way into Hamilton harbour, but they never found it! Every night there was a total blackout — it must have been a tense time. One bomb could have wiped out most of the Island chain, including service bases and people.

During the war no one ate well. One holiday my sister and I went for an overnight visit to a friend's place, but we had so little to eat I went home crying. The farms in Bermuda were the size of postage stamps, so everyone was tightly rationed. There were few treats, just one square of chocolate on Sundays! Christmas for years was very limited with few presents under the tree. One particular gift I remember well. That Christmas Dad had improvised, cutting an old crib in half, remodelling both ends so both my sister and I could have a doll's crib. I used to creep in to the living room very early Christmas morning and blow the trumpet ornaments and ring the bells ever so quietly. It was such a beautiful time to myself with the moonlight streaming through the window, glistening on the tree.

Bermuda had no cars so I went to school on the back of Dad's bike until I learned to ride. I remember one particular picnic was a big excursion by horse and carriage. The horse finally brought us home in the moonlight while we all slept, including the driver! Swimming was marvelous in Bermuda, and picnics included everything from lemon pie to squishy sandwiches made of tomatoes between fresh bread.

Dad was a busy minister. Mother used to say he was married to the church instead of to her. He didn't spend much time with us, and rarely made us things. One Easter my brother and I were outside in the backyard watching kites fly overhead. At times the string stretched right over our heads, almost close enough to touch. We were thrilled! On this particular afternoon we decided to pray that God would send us a kite. We went in behind the water tank, crouched down and prayed. It wasn't long before the string from a kite came down close enough for us to pull it into our yard. An answer to prayer! But a few moments later a little boy came to our gate crying and asked if anyone had seen his kite. Of course we gave it back. That taught me something about prayer!

In school I had little difficulty, being good with my hands and forced to do homework faithfully. The British system included weekly Scripture classes. Stories from the Old and New Testaments were read, so I learned most of my Bible knowledge in school. I used to love listening on a Friday afternoon as a teacher from Scotland read stories. I was the only one in class who could read that Bible stuff, as I had practiced and could get my tongue around the Thee's and Thou's!

When I turned twelve my parents let me have my one and only birthday party. Dad actually stayed home to run the games and was the life of the party! Otherwise we were always having to share our father with many other people. He had a daily morning radio devotional period, and was well known on the island. Many people spoke to him, and black children called him "Father." I never could figure that out. Wasn't he my father? Bermuda, at that time, was a segregated island. Black girls would throw stones at us as we peddled home from school. I remember that we had a coloured maid for a while, but she would never eat with us in the dining room, even though she was invited to do so.

The family revolved around mother; she was the hub of our lives, always there to greet us and help with projects. We were all spoiled, having everything done for us (except we had to make our beds Saturday mornings. This chore was lightened by a book hidden between mattress and floor.) Mother's domain was the kitchen, and we were not to get underfoot! My sister and I never did learn to cook or bake, which was a shame as mother could whip up a marvelous lemon pie with juicy Bermuda lemons off the tree. That pie was the birthday special in our family instead of a cake.

None of my school friends went to Dad's church, so I lived two lives. I didn't like either role because I always had to be careful not to ruin Dad's reputation. How I could do that escaped me, but one day when I was caught climbing in the church window in the middle of the Ministerial Association meeting, I almost did. I got it! That was probably spanking number two from Dad. He rarely disciplined us! I only remember three spankings. What we feared was mother and the cherry tree stick! From a very early age Mother's means of discipline was to get a twig from the cherry tree in the back yard and let us have it across the fingers. My brother and I used to break up every twig we found in the house! By the time mother had another, she had cooled off.

I have always been a deep feeler, saying little, going quietly about, keeping out of mischief. The war gave me many mixed feelings. The ships and their sailors docking on Front Street provided a treasure of exciting things to do. One ship from Portugal had a monkey on board as a mascot. I was broken-hearted on hearing that that ship had gone down.

The war years lasted until I was thirteen. The service men made the youth group at Church come alive. I enjoyed square dancing with them, and played the piano for the many Sunday evening sing songs. I loved music. From the day I saw the movie *Song To Remember*, on the life of Chopin, I wanted to be a concert pianist. I started practicing on the church piano in earnest, one hour every afternoon. I was going to be famous!

Comment: The Faith Gift in Spiral 4. "Life Stories"

My faith was moralistic at this time. We were never allowed to
go to movies, wear earrings, or put on lipstick — until my sister
rebelled. Dad rarely spent time with us, yet his wishes were always followed. I had to learn also that prayer didn't mean that
God would get me what I wished for. Faith wasn't magic.

I was fortunate in having Scripture in high school as a regular
part of the curriculum. I read the Bible in school as good litera-
ture and so got the basics for faith as book knowledge. My teachers were good story-tellers and gave me a love for many Bible
stories. I could listen for hours, and became a book worm.
Stories were where I learned about life, because my own life
was very cloistered.

I had to attend Church morning and evening every Sunday,
and Sunday School every Sunday afternoon at 3:00 p.m. Finally,
at the age of twelve, when I rebelled at attending so many services Dad asked me to be the organist for the evening service.

MY STORY IN SPIRAL 5
Inter-personal (Circa age twelve to fourteen)

Because my sister and I were not allowed many freedoms, my
teen years were very studious. Looking back, I think all I did
was go to school and go to church. My sense of self was all
mixed up with religion and what other people thought was
right. I didn't break away until I left the island to attend college.
Mother always said, "Wait until you go to college and then you
can go out with boys." I complied. There were always the other
young people in the church to do things with, but I didn't have
much to do outside the church. I feel this now as a hindrance,
but no doubt my parents were trying to protect me.

I think, on looking back, that the church expectations always
interfered with friendships. I was very protected, but didn't have
to be highly responsible like my older sister. This tended to
make her pushy, always telling me what to do, so I kept my dis-
tance. Being the middle child kept some of the parental expectations off my shoulders, but it was still hard living in a family

with such high expectations. They were never explicitly stated, but always implied and we were pushed hard. We were expected to amount to something and go to college. My sister got a scholarship, but I went to work in the Government Customs House for a year upon graduating from high school. There was a graduation dance, but I didn't go as I felt sure my Dad wouldn't approve. Anyway, I didn't know how to dance!

Comment: The Faith Gift in Spiral 5. "Forgiveness"

With this kind of church background, my faith had to grow along with what Dad and others expected of me. Forgiveness was always conditioned by first doing the right thing. I find it hard to this day to forgive myself when I've let someone down or done the wrong thing.

I remember an incident from this period that reflects my very high duty orientation. I was sick in bed one Sunday, listening to the Church School meeting next door in the church hall. They were singing the hymn:

"Trust and obey,
For there's no other way,
To be happy in Jesus,
But to trust and obey."

I heard this as a call from God and responded with a promise to trust and obey the Lord. I've never been sorry for this promise, but it certainly reflects a life controlled by something — there was no other way I knew of to be happy! I'd better obey!

The promise to obey the Lord meant there were lots of times I needed forgiveness for letting God and other people down. Even though my parents often said they forgave me this and that, God was another matter. Forgiveness, especially being able to forgive oneself, is basic for faith to grow. I've had to try to forgive myself all my life. I am still hard on myself though always able to forgive others as the "right" thing to do. It has been a struggle.

CHAPTER SEVEN

Life Beyond the Nest

MY STORY IN SPIRAL 6
Intra-Individual (Circa age fifteen to twenty-one)

The day finally came when I was to leave Bermuda to attend
college in Canada. I wanted to study music and be a concert
pianist. Dressed in new stockings, which I'd never worn before,
and with red flannel underwear packed in my suitcase, I flew
out of the nest, literally. Arriving at the Toronto airport was over-
whelming, and very exciting. I felt grown up at last and planned
on sharing an apartment with another girl from Bermuda who
was also a music student. I was seventeen and on an adventure!
Toronto was so fast! Running all that first week, either for a
street car or for a green light, made me stiff for days!

Life in Bermuda had spoiled me with its mild winters and
leisurely pace. The island is in the gulf stream, with semi-tropi-
cal weather. When I wanted to do something on a Saturday it
would be swimming with a friend, or going on a bicycle ride. I
never hung around the corner store or went to the movies.
Spending money was an unheard of treat. Now in Canada I had
a thousand dollars to last a year. That money represented years
of budgeting by Mom and Dad, and I spent it carefully. I was a
responsible kid, or tried to be. Still very dutiful!

It wasn't long before some of the glamour wore off. I had to
practice the piano six hours each day, Monday to Friday, which
left little time for housework. My roommate and I had a fight
over cleaning up! I was unhappy and looked for another place
to stay. The Deaconess School, where my sister was living, had

an extra room, so I moved in. This place was called The Missionary and Deaconess Training Home, and was run by the church. It's nickname was "The Angel Factory." Very sedate! No visitors in the Sitting Room and no boyfriends beyond the entrance way. It was an old, large, red brick house with beds for at least twenty girls and two bathrooms! I shared a room with two others. This place was very homey; however, the food wasn't like home. Home was gone for good. I was homesick for months.

But as time went on, most of us had a ball in that lovely old residence and I made many good friends. At first, being on my own and out from under Dad's reputation, I didn't go to church for the first year. Part of my adolescent rebellion? I suppose so. I was free! But now, here I was in the angel factory, or the Deac School, as some called the place, and not going to church was unheard of. So my sister and I started attending Calvin Church, and sang in the choir.

On Sunday, in those days you had to wear a hat, act in a ladylike way, and eat sandwiches served in the library for tea! Even with all the rules, this was a thrilling time in my life. I became quite a tease and enjoyed playing jokes. It wasn't beyond me to take a person's clothes away as they languished in the tub behind the screen and turn the old furnace overflow pipe down on them!

After a year at the Royal Conservatory of Music I began to have doubts. While practicing hour after hour in a little room at Knox Church, I was freezing even with heavy socks over my shoes! All this wasn't very encouraging. Was I really cut out to be a concert pianist in Canada? My hands also shook a lot when playing in public! After a night of soul searching, and on the prompting of my roommate, I decided to quit dreaming about being a concert pianist and decided to study towards becoming a Deaconess. I had heard what I thought was a divine call to serve the Church. Everyone was pleased, including my Dad and Mother. Later I was to wish I'd finished my music degree, but I thought I could easily combine music with a church position.

The Deaconess diploma course took three years. This included taking some courses at Knox Theological College. At

Knox our classes were separate from the men. We were told it was because we were undergraduates and didn't know Greek. But we were segregated in more ways than that. I'll tell you about that later.

During my first summer in Canada the whole family had a marvelous holiday together in Guelph. It was to be our last time together as a complete family. Dad had exchanged his church, pulpit, house, and car with the minister at St. Andrews and we all had a marvelous time. My brother and I learned to drive with that car and I almost crashed it! It's a wonder Dad allowed it, but I guess he wanted to teach us himself. Dad and I were both trying to get control of the steering wheel at the same time, sliding from one side to the other around a bend! I wonder if that moment is symbolic of my life with father.

The next year during the summer I accepted a posting as a student deaconess to Regina, Saskatchewan. This island girl took off for the wild and woolly West among the gophers on the prairies. I loved it, but I hadn't been there a month when I received a telegram with a Bible text on it. I don't remember what verse it was, but after consultation with my sister who was in Manitoba, we decided to fly home. Mother was very sick.

When I was 18, we lost Mother. Mom had always been there when I needed her and had written a letter every week, but I was careless in replying. No one knew how sick she was. Hypertension in those days was dangerous. A new drug was just coming on the market but it was too late to save her. While in hospital she kept asking to come home so Dad arranged it and tried to get a nurse. No private nurse was available, so my sister and I nursed mother until her death. We tried very hard but couldn't keep Mother alive. I'll never forget trying to clear her throat of phlegm and listening to her laboured breathing through the night. The hymn "The king of love my shepherd is" was sung at her funeral. It was years before I could sing that again! Even now, as I write, tears come to my eyes and a heaviness to my chest. Mother was dead at age 54.

I wonder now about the woman who was Mother. Did being a minister's wife get her down? Almost every Monday she had a headache. This educated, friendly, quiet woman encouraged her children to be all they could be. Mother had a violin but I never heard her play for the heat dried out the glue, and it fell apart. This violin was in my possession for years until I sold it to pay for a guitar. I felt guilty about that! After Mother died nothing was the same. Even the dog Rusty, our cocker spaniel, was hard to handle. My brother had a real hard time adjusting to mother's death and only years later did my grief catch up with me. Meanwhile, I stayed home for a year to look after Dad.

I will always regret not knowing Mother as an adult, one to one. She died too soon, just when we were all leaving and going off to college. Perhaps she felt useless? Nursing her at the end gave me a chance to say thank you. After a year, I was pleased that Dad married a woman in the congregation whom we all knew well. I played the organ for their wedding and returned to Canada on the same flight with them. Our suitcases got mixed and the bride got a suitcase of my books. I wonder who did that?

Back at the Deac School I had a year's studies to catch up on, and all the pressure finally proved too much. I landed in the hospital with a suspected brain tumour — it was scary. One day, looking down from the hospital window to the street below, I wondered if I'd ever walk out there again. In the end, I learned I'd had an emotional breakdown. A good rest at my sister's apartment (she had married by then) put me back on my feet. This whole episode gave me a lot of thinking and praying time, but no counselling. Few understood such things in those days, and I didn't realize I had buried my grief for Mother when I should have expressed it.

Comment: The Faith Gifts in Spiral 6. "Acceptance of Difference"

So much happened in my life between the ages of 17 to 21. This was a demanding transition time that had a lasting impression on my faith. Faith had been quite conventional before, and I stayed away from church when I could. At first I didn't want to accept things the way they were. I had rebelled at housework! I had tried hard to keep mother alive! Finally, in that hospital room, thinking I had a brain tumour, my faith became more personal. There was nowhere else to turn. I had never really thrown Christianity out the window, but had rebelled at having to attend church all the time. Mother's death was extremely painful, but I did not blame God. God meant too much to Dad to do that! My upbringing taught me to turn to Dad and the church for safety. Everywhere else was dangerous. Church and home were my security. God and my father were all mixed up as protective role models. I now turned to God.

During these years I had a recurring nightmare of black gowns chasing me. The only way I could get away was to fly high into the sky, which I did, and escaped every time. (Now, as a minister myself, I will not wear a black gown! Mine is white, with a blue cloak.) Later I got to know the man behind the black gown, but at that time it was pretty hard trying to please all those black gowns. I was embedded in churchy systems and trying to get away to be myself. I was searching for myself even as my body was rebelling, trying to get out from under Dad's shadow.

Using Erikson's concept of the developmental tasks, we could say that this spiral represents the struggle between identity and identity confusion. So many different things were happening to me — it really shook me up. Into this confusion came the friends from the Deac School, visiting me in the hospital, assuring me that they cared. I was accepted as a person and learned to accept things I couldn't change, or at least started to. The faith gift in this spiral, the acceptance of difference, reached out to me through all the changes. Mother was gone, Dad was far away. My friends lifted me out of despair and got me going again. The struggle with my health led me to accept the differences in my life, this new life in Canada.

CHAPTER EIGHT

Life in the Church

MY STORY IN SPIRAL 7
Intro-vocational (Circa age twenty-two to twenty-nine)

All through my college years I was careful not to push myself too hard; a headache was enough to make me slow up. I was nervous and tense, living on phenobarbitol and drumming my fingers on the arm rest of every chair. I couldn't sit still.

Back at the Deaconess School and taking classes at Knox College I was finding out what it meant to be just a woman in the church. They barely tolerated us. As recently as 1984, while involved in a residential program held in another seminary, I noticed the bathroom provisions for the women were inadequate. It was obvious that having women around was just barely tolerated. I blew up in that place! Looking back, I realize that the surroundings brought back memories of Knox College in the '50s. I must have been very angry then too, but true to form, I kept quiet.

There is still a lot of anger in me over what happened to women in the church in the '40s and '50s. I had been brought up with the idea I could be anything I wanted to be, but then at Knox, I didn't fit in. It is different there now, but back then I seemed to be experiencing this isolation often. When would I ever fit in? As student Deaconesses we were not allowed to talk with the guys in the halls. When girls got married they couldn't even work in the Deaconess Order, so fraternizing was discouraged. A married woman's place was in the kitchen.

While attending classes at Knox, the student Deacs often went to worship in the lovely chapel, but were only allowed to sit in the last two pews on the left. The men sat forward, anywhere in front of us, and the professors sat scattered on the right! The time came when I got a chance to change this. I could play the magnificent organ in the chapel, and they asked me if I would play for chapel services. I said I wouldn't go way up front in the chapel unless all the girls could move up and sit anywhere on the left. So I played and they moved forward! A small victory, perhaps, but it helped to ease the feelings of subordination. This story illustrates only too well what happened to us for years as professional women in the church!

Women have been ordained in the Presbyterian Church in Canada since 1967, ordained to both the preaching, and ruling ministries in the eldership. Everything is changing slowly. Now many women attend Presbytery and the other courts of the church, but the transition has left scars on loyal women, while others just left. I can still feel many of these unresolved tensions in me.

The first positions I had as a Deaconess, working as a Director of Christian Education in various churches, were not particularly happy ones. Those churches couldn't afford both a Deaconess and a secretary so I was both. I hadn't trained to be a secretary and couldn't type well. Looking back, I realize that working as a Deaconess was not the right position for me in the church. I never fitted in too well working under the direction of a minister; I wasn't good at taking orders. If it wasn't the minister, it was the Ladies' Aid president telling me off for something.

One day, while preparing for a children's group in a church in Montreal, I carelessly left a pot on the stove full of melting wax. It was turned way down, but the pot dissolved and the melted wax went all over the stove. What a mess and what an irate woman who found it! It was the president of the Ladies' Aid and I had goofed badly in her domain, the kitchen! She was furious.

While working as a Deaconess there didn't seem to be room for me to grow as a person. Things finally came to a head in a church in Ontario and I got fired. Several churches were promoting an ecumenical teacher's institute, and I was being interviewed by the press. I've no idea what I actually told the reporter but what appeared as a headline in the newspaper was, TEACHERS CALLED DEPLORABLE. The whole primary staff of the church school quit, and I was told that I was out of a job. Where could I go, what could I do? I was totally fed up with churches. I cried for days.

In those days, Sessions and Presbyteries were composed entirely of men. They would sit in the court, dressed in their best black suits and white shirts, looking like a bunch of penguins. Solemnly they sat, staring at me, sort of ruffling, flexing their wings. When I approached such a severe court of the church and asked for a hearing, I knew I just didn't fit in. I can remember going to the church where Presbytery was meeting, hoping to get a hearing, but on peaking through the door at this august bunch, I fled!

The Board of Missions came to my rescue and sent me where I was really needed, to northern Alberta and the Peace River Country. So began my travel adventures and a new life. Two friends were going out west on a camping trip across Canada that summer and very kindly took me with them. We headed north, camping in farmers' fields and along river banks. Mile by mile we crossed the prairies, going through the United States. One night we camped by the Missouri River and at sunrise, as was our custom, we spent a few moments off by ourselves in private devotions. I was sitting by the river reading the Bible, feeling sorry for myself, thinking that I was going off into the middle of nowhere. Then the sun came up and a warmth filled me that was far stronger than the natural warmth of the early sun. I knew it was God's love filling me and that I would not be alone in the Peace River. I don't remember saying anything about this experience to my friends for I am quiet about such things, but I've never forgotten. That moment with the Lord changed my life. The early morning sun opened me to the Holy Spirit's presence, and I've never felt alone since.

On arriving in Fort St. John we tried to make contact with the superintendent of missions, whom we had heard was a very large man, and we figured we had found him when we saw the clothes on the line outside the Manse! That first Sunday he and I were driving to Chetwyn, crossing the mountains to take an af-

ternoon service, when he asked me if I would preach. This man
had a reputation as a tease, so I thought he was putting me on.
"I've never preached before," I said, "but if you will be quiet for
thirty minutes I'll put something together." I've always been
willing to try anything once and he took me up on it! So I gave
my first sermon in that little log church, using the Psalm "Unto
the hills around will I lift up my longing eyes." It was a personal
description of the trip West, and of my need to find my place.

When we finally got to the church camp that evening, I discovered I was to sleep on a wooden bunk bed with straw for a
mattress. I knew by this time that the Peace River was either going to make me or break me! I was placed in the church in
Grand Prairie, going to two other country churches most Sundays and through it all, had a great time. In the Peace it wasn't a
hindrance to be a woman, and an outspoken one at that! The
church people welcomed me with open arms, and at last I be-
longed. I discovered that I'm a pioneer at heart.

Later that winter, while driving the same mountain road to
Chetwyn, my car skidded on a curve, leaving me stranded with
the front wheels over the edge. I didn't dare move or the car
would go right over and tumble down the mountain side. I
carefully turned off the motor and sat there praying. This was a
deserted mountain road and I didn't know what to do. No more
than ten minutes had passed when a big logging truck came
'round the curve, stopped, and carefully pulled me off. I was
safe! Thank the Lord! I went down the mountain and stopped
in at a café for a cup of hot chocolate, shaking all the way,
thankful to God that I was alive!

I loved it in the North, and could listen by the hour to the
tales of pioneer days. Many people could still remember the
hard trip in. One dear old soul whom I visited regularly told me
of how they struggled to bring in their piano over the cord
roads. These roads were tree trunks laid side by side through
the muskeg. The horse pulled the wagon wheels, bump by
bump, across cord by cord. Going up hills with a piano in the
covered wagon was tough, so they made two trips, unloading
the piano at the top and returning for the rest of the load. I sat

down and played her piano. She loved the gospel song "Beyond the Sunset"!

Comment: The Faith Gift in Spiral 7. "Love"

Few incidents have affected my faith as much as those that happened by the river and on the mountain road, where I learned that prayer is answered, and God is love. This spiral was full of crises that tested my faith in myself and my desire to serve the Lord within the church.

I had many friends throughout this period, but during my twenties few people got beneath the Deaconess veneer of competence, independence, and church worker *extraordinaire*. I figured nothing was too hard for me to tackle but it took an experience with the Lord's love to fill me with warmth for people.

There were few single men in those churches, but there was one that I really liked but he was as shy as I was. Another had a small plane and was teaching me to fly. I often asked God to send a man into my life who would be interested in serving the Lord with me. Yet I would always say that I would never marry a minister! I'm still single, for most men I got to know were more interested in a woman being in the kitchen than in the church! But my life has never been lonely, for it has been full of people, all giving me much love. Love was understood primarily as love for God first, others second (men), and self last. Surely the faith gift in this spiral is love. No one can live and grow in faith without it. God's love reaches us in many ways, directly and through loving people who reach out to us.

MY STORY IN SPIRAL 8
Intro-world (Circa age thirty to thirty-nine)

When I left the Peace River it was to take up a position in Red Deer, Alberta. The minister there told me, "Wash that gumbo off your car, you're back in civilization now!" I was to start a church in the new suburban area of West Park. The Presbytery had obtained a temporary hall and set it up on blocks. The church downtown gave me twelve names to visit; these families became my twelve "disciples" and attended the first service. The congregation and church school grew until we were strong enough to hold our first bazaar. I'll never forget that day! The water wouldn't run and someone said to get the fire department to thaw the pipes. We phoned and the big red fire truck arrived for tea at the same time as the paying guests!

The years in Red Deer were happy ones as long as the tables attached to the wall didn't collapse during Sunday School, or the portable organ's legs didn't give out during church! It was fun in the little hall and people were drawn to the fledgling congregation. At one time my Dad came out on holiday and baptized six babies — I was not allowed to officiate at the sacraments because I wasn't ordained. But I did everything else and was happy doing ministry.

The day came when this congregation needed a permanent church building. The Presbytery felt they should ask for an ordained minister to carry on the work. To ease the separation I went to live in the Eckville manse for the last year and took the services at both churches. The Eckville congregation was meeting in the basement of their unfinished church. The story got around that it took a woman to get those farmers to finish the sanctuary, and they did! It is a lovely little church. The men did a great job and I am good friends with many of those families to this day. But by now I was thinking that I should be ordained, as I was tired of being pushed out by a male minister just when things got interesting. This meant going back to college. So I made arrangements to go to Winnipeg to attend college again, this time for a B.A., further studies in theology, and finally, ordination. By then the church had voted to ordain women.

Attending college in Winnipeg and being a student again got sort of boring. I ran out of money, so I asked to be put back to work as a Deaconess. For about a year I was part-time Deac in the Presbytery, helping in the Christian Education program of various churches. During the second year there, besides studying, I helped start an inner-city mission with another Deaconess. We moved in to an old house by the Arlington Railway Bridge and invited the children of the area to join different clubs.

At its peak, Flora House, as we called the mission, had over 150 children each week. The children came after school on different days depending on their age. They would participate in a varied program of stories, crafts, and games. People from local churches helped us and provided refreshments. This was a Christian program and it made all of us happy to see the children feel so much at home. We were there for the boy who brought in a bird with a broken wing, and for a child unable to get into her locked home. We settled fights and showed by example that we cared! Flora House taught me that faith must be practical. I felt then that ordination to the ministry wouldn't help with those kids, as most of them wouldn't darken a church door, so I put ordination on the back burner for a while and took eight years to get my B.A.

These children were adorable but tough. As a protected, middle-class minister's daughter I needed to be toughened up! I had never before seen a baby sleeping in the bottom drawer of the bedroom dresser because there was no other place for him. I got to know one of the boys who was too scared to go home to his alcoholic mother, or to face a beating from his father. Instead he would sit on the corner rug in our living room never saying a word, just looking sad. The children taught me about life on the other side of the tracks, where "Jesus" was a swear word.

One of the best programs we ever held was the Christmas Pageant. This was a big production held in the sanctuary of one of the local churches with our children taking all the parts. They did beautifully! Tears were often in our eyes as the angels paraded up the aisle and child-like Mary sang the *Magnificat* with so much joy. It was worth all the work to see their sparkling eyes in the candlelight. Most Canadian Christmases have lots of presents under a decorated tree, but not for some of those families. The present received from Santa at Flora House was often the only one and had to be carefully rewrapped for Christmas morning.

After eight years in Winnipeg I finally obtained my B.A. degree and it was time to move on. I was very tired, looking out for the children during the day and writing essays after 10:00

p.m. I was exhausted physically and emotionally, and so was my partner. We split up and I took off for Sabbatical leave in the Californian sun.

Comment: The Faith Gift in Spiral 8. "Caring"

The experience at Flora House with all those children, all so needy, was a time of awakening. The opportunity to care for children and to help them each day as they came home from school meant my parenting urge was filled. I put heart and soul into caring for them, trying to alleviate some of their hurting. Caring about those children strengthened my faith. This opportunity to care was a precious gift to this detached, middle-class minister's daughter. It allowed me to be someone who got involved with social issues, trying to make some worthwhile changes. Surely the opportunity to care that those children offered me was a gift, helping me grow in faith.

MY STORY IN SPIRAL 9
Extra-self (Circa age forty to fifty-five)

It was time for some long-delayed sabbatical leave. On arriving at the Los Angeles airport, I rented a car and drove through that maze of freeways to find the Claremont School of Theology. There I spent a couple of years studying and loved every minute of it.

This period of study was a pivotal time in my life. The course with Dr. Howard Clinebell, "Training Laymen for Pastoral Care and Social Action," included lab work with a small group in a local church. My group experience was marvelous. For the first time in my life I was treated as just plain "Iris," not as a minister's daughter or Deaconess. I thoroughly enjoyed the sharing as the group tried to discover together what it meant to put the Christian faith into loving action, and really do something to help when someone was hurting. The group experience excited me, and I decided that this way of sharing faith and action was what was missing in the church. We talk a lot about love in churches, but where is it? Here was the answer! In a small group of not more than twelve people, everyone could get to know each other well enough to be truly supportive. Meeting in small faith-sharing groups, as well as in congregational worship, church members could become what they are supposed to be, a loving fellowship. I now thought I had all the answers to the problem with the church!

I followed up this good experience with a year-and-a-half in El Cajon, working in a church as the assistant minister. I continued my studies (in the same area of counselling through small groups) to fulfill student visa requirements. Again, the group experience was positive.

By this time I wanted to stay in California so I applied for ordination, and made out an application for permanent residency. However, God had other ideas! I took seriously ill and after major surgery was let go from my church position. This was the second time in my life that I was fired from a church! You'd think I'd learn someday!

CHAPTER NINE

Life Through Crises

The drive back to Canada in my weakened physical condition and my angry emotional state was something else. As usual, I never divulged my true feelings to my friend who was driving me home to British Columbia where my father and stepmother lived. I've always hidden most of my bad feelings from other people as much as possible, trying to be a strong Christian in good times and bad.

While recovering in Haney with my parents I got to know and appreciate them again. I exercised every day, hooked a rug for diversion, and edited the tapes from the Claremont School's small group sessions. I hoped to recuperate over the winter, and wrote a book on small groups. Beyond that I didn't know what I wanted to do, being confused about people, the church, and myself.

When I had my strength and equilibrium back I found it hard to settle down. All I had ever done was church work. Now, during an interview with manpower, I found I wasn't trained for anything else. Finally, I took a summer job as a Deaconess again on Vancouver Island. I enjoyed living on an island again, but this experience showed me that I really was not happy working as a Deaconess.

It was decision time about employment. What did life offer me? I knew now that I still wanted to serve Christ in some way, but did it have to be in the employ of a church? Freelancing was the answer. So I made myself available doing small groups in various churches throughout the lower mainland of British Columbia. Eventually, an ecumenical organization gave me a desk and telephone and I found myself contacting hundreds of fine people who were also searching for a viable faith and needing help with spiritual growth. Starting small groups and writing, I continued to freelance for two years, but I never knew where the next dollar was coming from. Each day was amazing — enough love gifts would always come in. I learned to trust my life in faith. God would provide through the people I was helping in various small groups. I quit worrying about the next day's needs, though it was always hard on my stomach not knowing when the next money would appear.

I shared an apartment with a friend during this time. We were good for each other, both being in a transition period. She was in the mid-twenty crisis and I was in the mid-forty one!

Comment: The Faith Gift in Spiral 9. "Acceptance of limits"

During this transitional time in my life, faith in the institutional church took a bad beating, and barely survived. Faith in myself also took a beating, but came through stronger in the end. Faith in the Lord kept me going! I prayed for my return to health and some healthy balance in my life. Indeed, at that time I probably blamed my personal struggle on my health, and thought if I could just feel better everything would be O.K. again. I had always thought that the Lord required hard work, and things only went out of control (my control) when I got sick. So I prayed for health. I had not considered that the reason for poor health could well be my attitude towards God and myself, in that I tended to see faith as "duty." This transition took me from always trying to serve others and do my duty back into the inner journey to find wholeness within.

Following Erikson's development tasks, we saw that the psychosocial task of this spiral was the balancing of integrity with despair. In my mid-forties, looking back at my life and my health, I was in despair. Service to God through the church no longer was credible. Where was my integrity? Could I accept the need to change when I saw little hope of the church changing? Into all this came the awareness that I needed to accept my limits and to accept what I couldn't change in the church. In the personal struggle, many people helped me accept myself, weaknesses and all; they gave a lasting gift to me that has strengthened my faith ever since.

MY STORY IN SPIRAL TEN
Spiritual (Circa age fifty-five to sixty-five)

During my stay in Vancouver my friend and I shared an apartment that had a lovely view of Kitsilano Beach and the downtown skyline of Vancouver. Every day it was our practice to share devotions together. On one particular day as my friend was reading Scripture, I had a strange experience that moved me deeply. I've never let people tag me with "charismatic" as I don't like being labeled. However, on this occasion it was as if water was being poured on my head and all through me. It probably only lasted for a few seconds, but it felt like being in the shower and all the tension was washed out of my body. For me this was an experience of the cleansing, healing power of the Spirit flowing through my emotions.

The next day I started to cry, ever so gently. I cried all day and when asked why I was crying, I didn't know. Looking back, I knew. I was crying all the tears never shed over mother's death. I was being cleansed of the effects of grief and released from the pain harboured since my twenties. This was a unique experience for me, and now I know the loving power that heals at a deep personal level. This "releasing within" has continued, so that I now do not harbour grief or try to carry another's pain, but I share it with God.

There was another profound change in my life as I entered this spiral. I do not whip myself mentally anymore, or stay awake nights trying to analyze the day. When I do something wrong now, like letting someone down, or failing in what I feel God wants me to do, I know that healing and divine forgiveness are always available on request. I can forgive myself more easily now. Looking back I can see that every time life has crushed me, faith gifts have lifted me up and carried me through. I had received the faith gift of letting go and letting God. But I can also say that God takes plenty of time coming to my rescue!

The Ministry at Last

How many times had I considered being ordained to the Christian ministry? I've lost count, but if the Presbyterian Church had ordained women back in my twenties I still don't think I would have been ready then. The road I've travelled has made me a very different minister.

The Presbytery of Vancouver asked General Assembly to ordain me to the special ministry of adult spiritual growth within the Vancouver area. I was disappointed when the ruling was to take a year of theology at Knox College in Toronto. So I packed my bags and drove East — it was study time again. I had so far spent 13½ years in some form of post-high school education, but I took three more semesters and finally accomplished the M.Div. degree and ordination.

Despite no money (once again!) things worked out and God's leading was obvious. A wiser head than mine was planning each move. In Toronto I found a place to stay with a woman who has since become a dear friend. She needed someone to help look after her elderly aunt. Staying with them was like having a home away from home. When my student loan money ran out another miracle of timing occurred. An old Bermuda friend of the Ford family died and left me enough money to live on until I finished studying at Knox. I knew nothing of this legacy ahead of time, but it came through just when I needed financial help. I seemed to be experiencing faith at a deeper level, beyond my control. The burden for figuring out my choices in life seemed lighter, but I still worked hard. There was a difference in my attitude now; I didn't worry so much about things working out.

On graduation from Knox I told the General Board of Missions that I would serve in an extension area, starting a brand new church. I thought that in a new situation there would be more opportunity and freedom for me to be myself. I wouldn't have to fit in to a settled, masculine model of ministry. Out of several possible areas I chose Waterloo, but ordination was in Dad's previous church in New Westminster. Dad gave the Charge to the Ordinand — a pep talk to the new minister —

and everyone was in tears. When I got up to give the Benediction I heard my voice come out all squeaky, high-pitched with emotion. Ordination was a high for my spirit — I had finally come home spiritually.

Comment: The Faith Gift in Spiral 10. "Letting go"

Ordination was a peak moment in my life. I had felt, right up to the last moment, that I would be revealed as the sinner I was, and wouldn't be ordained. I've never felt good enough for such moments, but loving friends have shown me to be open about my weaknesses. This honesty also makes it possible for people to identify with my goals, and we all learn from our failures. No longer do I try to be a super Christian, forcing people to give in to my presumed strengths. I am still a very private person, but now I know that true ministry is through humility, not pride of accomplishment. In weakness, even sickness, my soul has grown over the years.

I was now officially appointed to the new parish of Waterloo North and installed by the Presbytery. I resolved to share ministry with my congregation, trying always to make room around me for other people to exercise their talents in a shared ministry. Building a new church almost did me in but we have a lovely congregation, and I am still with them. Through all of this I think I have learned to let go and let God, though sometimes I catch myself carrying all the load as if I were alone again. Letting go has not meant giving up, but it has given me the freedom to try again without worrying so much about how the results will look to others.

In Waterloo North Church my ministry style is very different from the time I started the church in Red Deer. Both tasks were the same: to start a new church. Then I pushed myself and others like mad, but now, even though I don't push other people the way I used to, I seem to get much more done. When I get going in the old way, pushing myself and others, we all seem to be out of step with destiny and things just don't go right!

The problem with churches is how to get organized in a way

that leaves people free to be themselves. Too often a certain doctrine or program is insisted upon, which leave no room for personal spiritual growth. Too often people are made to fit into certain jobs just because there is a vacancy, not because they are suited or interested. They do their duty by the church! This fixes them in Spiral 6 and limits their growth in faith.

The church in Waterloo has built a shared sanctuary with an Anglican congregation, and our membership has grown. It has been a stretching experience, sharing a church building while retaining separate services. Then four years ago, I fell and broke my hip. Here was another physical setback. Would everything fall apart as it did when I couldn't keep pushing before and I got fired? It didn't! The congregation was strengthened and so was I. But that would have really thrown me ten years ago. This time I didn't get terribly depressed, stretched out for six weeks on my couch, day after day. I did what I could, talking on the phone, and even giving sermons from a chair with the elders conducting the rest of the service. Together we managed, and faith was strengthened all round.

MY STORY IN SPIRAL ELEVEN
Transitional (Circa sixty-five to seventy-five)

Sorry, I haven't reached this spiral yet, but I am already identifying with the saying, "Now what?"

CHAPTER TEN

Unfolding Spirals

A few questions remain in my mind. How do spirals unfold? Are they always sequential and connected, fixed in a predetermined order, as in stage theory? Are faith gifts developmental? Is there a negative route? Can spirals be compressed, speeded up, so that a person can be in spiral 12 at age 33, like Jesus, or do spirals always unfold naturally, determined by maturation?

Spirals are sequential in that they do build on the maturation process, but in my experience faith goes up and down like a yo-yo. Spirals can go off in a tangent, be out of balance, quickened, or even go in reverse. Also, faith gifts are repeatable opportunities. So faith spirals are not fixed, nor are they hierarchical. A faith spiral is not a once-for-all-time stage in life, they are repeatable with faith gifts reaching us again and again. The only draw back is that faith gifts may not be as easily appropriated in a later spiral.

Since each spiral represents a period of maximum openness to a particular faith gift, it is a person's openness that forms the pattern of the spiral, not a pre-determined, sequential series of stages. Each faith gift does depend to some extent on the appropriation of previous gifts. There is a progression, for instance, from trust as the basis of everything to joy deepening when trust is there. A sense of O.K.ness blossoms with joy in oneself. Through stories shared, a child is introduced to the worth in another's life, and forgiveness makes it possible to get close. Forgiveness is the basis for acceptance of differences between people which allows for love of someone who is different. Love reaches out to the "other," and understands and accepts differences.

As relationships mature love becomes a deep caring for the loved one, and acceptance of limits makes it possible to keep loving by letting go of those things one cannot change. The faith gift of renewal of hope broadens the person's horizons even when physical limits are imposed. Finally, the gift of peace expands with the acceptance of all previous gifts, but especially with the gifts of accepting of limits, and hope. So, the Spiral Faith model does reveal a sequential pattern unfolding in faith gifts.

Some people seem to reject faith gifts or at best only appropriate them halfheartedly. What has happened? We need to look carefully at the opposite of faith, the negation of faith gifts. When faith is "that which gives meaning to life," then the rejection of faith gifts, or the inability to appropriate faith gifts, is that which disrupts meaning, or destroys life. Yet few people actually destroy their lives, most seem to appropriate faith gifts at varying levels of intensity. A person tends to reject absolutes, leaving themselves a bit of room to maneuver. For instance, on a scale of 1-10 most people place their trust level near the middle, seeing themselves as average.

          1 2 3 4 5 6 7 8 9 10
Trust _____ Distrust

It is possible to identify the antithesis to each faith gift, but please keep in mind that these are not absolutes. They are misappropriation of faith gifts at varying intensities.

Spiral Embeddedment	Faith Gift	Misappropriation
1. Family	Trust	Distrust
2. Feelings	Joy	Grief
3. Needs	O.K.ness	Not O.K.
4. Skills	Life stories	Disinterest
5. Mutuality	Forgiveness	Accusations
6. Cultural systems	Acceptance of difference	Rejection of difference

7. Discipleship	Love	Hate
8. Stewardship	Caring	Not caring
9. Experience	Acceptance of Limits	Striving
10. Perspective	Letting go	Holding on
11. Change	Hope	Bitterness
12. Faith	Peace	Anxiety

It can be seen that the misappropriation of faith gifts turns a person in on self. These negative choices are the antithesis of openness. They speak loud and clear of SHUT-DOWN! Also, every choice a person makes is relative, with many influences affecting the decision. One of the most influential is the condition of embeddedment in a person's life. For example: where the embeddedness in spiral two is parental child abuse, and a kind neighbour, who does not know the situation at home hugs the child, there will be withdrawal. This child will not be able to open up to joy being unable to believe there is trust or love in

Embedded-ment	Faith Gifts	Psychosocial	Virtue/Vice
Family	Trust	Basic trust/ mistrust	Hope/gluttony
Feelings	Joy	Autonomy/ shame, doubt	Will/anger
Needs	O.K.ness	Initiative/guilt	Purpose/greed
Skills	People's stories	Industry/ inferiority	Competence/ envy
Mutuality	Forgiveness	Affiliation/ abandonment	
Cultural systems	Acceptance of difference	Identity/identity confusion	Fidelity/ pride
Discipleship	Love	Intimacy/ isolation	Love/lust
Stewardship	Caring	Generativity/ stagnation	Care/ indifference
Experience	Acceptance of limits	Integrity/ despair	Wisdom/ melancholy
Perspective	Letting go	Interiority/ separation	
Change	Hope	Expanding/ constricting	
Faith	Peace	Trust/Fear	

the hug. Throughout life openness to faith gifts depends on the health in the embeddedness situation in each spiral.

The following table shows the embeddedness situation and the faith gifts with their corresponding psychosocial task in each psychosocial task. This table also shows a list of virtues and vices which directly affect faith choices. The virtues are taken from Erik Erikson's essay "Human Strength and the Cycle of Generations."[1] Donald C. Capp in *Life Cycle Theory and Pastoral Care* provides the list of vices.[2]

This chart indicates the many possible negative choices affecting growth in faith throughout life! Each of the situations listed under embeddedment and psychosocial task influence growth in subsequent spirals. It is very important that ways of strengthening the embeddedment situation, and balancing the psychosocial task in each spiral be found. Openness to faith gifts is affected by everything that happens in the family, street, school, sports arena, college, the work place, neighbourhood centres, and places of worship. Everything possible should be done to strengthen the person's positive experience in each one.

Sadly, there are many people walking the negative path, following a continuous spiral that is in the process of shutting down, literally. For example, a person who has not resolved the conflict between industry and inferiority during the school years will try to resolve it all through life, continuously pushing himself or herself. Such a person may be desperate for help but unable to recognize it when help is given. He or she would never dare reach out on one's own and usually ends up blaming others, or God, for lack of support. Any inability to resolve the conflict between the psychosocial tasks will negate growth, affecting the acceptance of all subsequent faith gifts.

Evelyn and James Whitehead in their excellent book, *Christian Life Patterns*,[3] discuss how patterns that seem to be fixed can be changed. They use many good illustrations and give fascinating insights into human behaviour. Faith has many resources for change. One should not give up.

Donald Capp has also considered the effect of negative choices on growth. He has made a few changes in the ancient

list of "The Seven Deadly Sins," and though the concept of sin is
not fashionable today, he helps us realize that all these vices are
negative choices that shut down the personality. A person has a
major growth problem when vices, or sins, affect all future
growth in faith. Vices literally bring about closure of the personality. Donald Capp also refers us to Erikson's interesting description of the counterparts to virtues:

> From the infancy stage through mature adulthood
> these antipathies are withdrawal, compulsion, inhibi-
> tion, inertia, repudiation, exclusivity, rejection and
> disdain.[4]

It is obvious that Erikson and other sociologists view growth
of any kind as greatly hindered if the personality is in a state of
withdrawal. The extent of withdrawal and its effect on appropriation of faith gifts would vary with every person; it is doubtful
that anyone is completely open or completely closed. This
means, though, that few people are fully maturing in faith, for
few are completely open to grace.

A person can gain from the Spiral Faith model some idea of
the growth possible in the faith journey. But knowledge is usually not enough. There also needs to be a continuous response
to the creative call in life to reach out for the unknown and not
yet experienced, to live life to the fullest. James Fowler talks of
the human vocation as responding to God's call to become
partners in God's work in the world.

> What does it mean to be a mature human being? In
> what pursuit or devotion lies the fulfillment of hu-
> man potential? What is the shape of human comple-
> tion and wholeness? Christian faith, in its classic story
> and vision, tells us that human fulfillment means to
> recognize that we are constituted by the address and
> calling of God and to respond so as to become part-
> ners in God's work in the world.[5]

This call involves nothing less than a person's spiritual search for self in relation with the universe. The Christian believes that this search finds its ultimate answer in God as revealed through Jesus Christ. God calls a person to experience ultimate meaning and equips that person through the faith gifts. Faithing, then, is a person's answer to their creation. Made in the image of God, a person can reach for the ultimate, to live by the attributes of God: trust, joy, O.K.ness, the offer of salvation, forgiveness, acceptance, love, caring, the acceptance of limits, the freedom of letting go, the renewal of hope and peace. Through the faith gifts, or God's spirit touching a person's life, it is possible to grow in faith throughout the life cycle.

Depending on our responses to this call to live fully, faith spirals unfold in either a positive or negative pattern. Faith gifts influence a positive pattern; their rejection influences a negative pattern.

Each person has so many choices! One friend illustrated the dilemma this way: "Life is a route which we travel with many forks in the road. Growth is often involved with the vital choice. What should I do? Which way should I go? What choice should I make? I make a negative decision, but how long I stay on the negative route, as I fight my way back, is the important question that affects my ability to be open. People don't grow because they are not open to the risks at the fork in the road." Openness means risk! Growth in faith takes courage.

Footnotes
[1]Erik H. Erikson, *Insight and Responsibility* (New York: W. W. Norton, 1964).
[2]Donald Capps, *Life Cycle Theory and Pastoral Care* Ed. Don S. Browning (Philadelphia: Fortress Press, 1983), p. 37ff.
[3]Evelyn E. Whitehead and James D. Whitehead, *Christian Life Patterns. The Psychological Challenges and Religious Invitations of Adult Life* (New York: Image Books. Doubleday, 1982).
[4]Erik H. Erikson *Life Cycle Completed* (New York: W. W. Norton, 1982) p. 35.
[5]James W. Fowler, *Becoming Adult, Becoming Christian: Adult Development and Christian Faith* (San Francisco: Harper & Row, 1984), p. 92.

CHAPTER ELEVEN

Spirals and the Church

Several people have questioned whether the Spiral Faith Model is Christian. After all, there is no scripture given to substantiate any of the assumptions. Yet, Biblical truths are everywhere in this book. Faithing is a person's response to the gift of God's grace, the gift of God's love given in blessing. Growth in faith is the result of a person's ever-deepening response to spiritual stimulation and results in eventual union with the Creator of all life, God. Does the Spiral Faith Model mean that Christ is a process instead of a person and a foundation? Surely Christ's gift of salvation is the basic gift that gives life meaning: God in humanity! Jesus is the ultimate example of the faith-walk in union with God.

Faith is impossible without awareness of a call from beyond to reach for the ultimate. It includes faith in oneself, true, but that can grow only when one's life is seen in a larger framework than the self. Faith, then, is the journey that transcends self. Faith for all of life has about it a dimension of belief in the unknown, of reaching for that which goes beyond experience. Faithing is the ever-widening response of the person to life. Faith is coming to know that "It is O.K. to be alive!"

Faith as meaning-making implies a certain perspective on life. There is a searching for wisdom, a need for understanding, a longing to "know" one's end. The person who focuses for meaning only in the "nowness" of life sets only short-term goals, temporal goals like money, a home and family, success on the job. This is not taking the perspective that life itself is a gift from God and returns to God. There may be a feeling of rootlessness when temporal goals are accomplished. Making-meaning of ALL of life, even birth and death, is the purpose of the faith journey.

This faith journey is not totally individual, although it is personal; a person is part of a community. Faith's growth is imbedded in community, and faithing is shared. There is little growth when faith is kept to oneself. As growth in faith takes place within the community, emphasis should be placed on the quality of that embeddedment. This model should have a profound effect on church life, on teaching, and preaching. Sermons could use illustrations and insights that would present faith needs from the perspective of two or three spirals, not just from Spiral 12, making everyone feel inadequate! Preachers tend to ask why so few in the congregation are spiritually mature, instead of presenting opportunities for growth in faith.

The Spiral Faith Model also shows why so many people over the age of 50 are in the churches. They are in that spiral where transcendent truth becomes personalized. The model also shows why young adults continuously complain that few worship services touch them personally. Relationships, feelings of intimacy with the Lord and other people, are vital in this spiral. Church music and services for teens and young adults should reflect their need for more passion in worship.

This model for growth in faith does give rise to questions about standard church practice with such age-related events as confirmation, and conversion. At ages 12-16 the teenager is embedded in the peer group and will be confirmed because others are doing it. They will relate to the church as to their family or peers, as to a cultural system, thinking they have to fit in. They are not ready to relate intimately with Christ in conversion. That comes in Spiral 7, or around age 18 or later. A church is justified in inviting teenagers into church at confirmation as the place they belong spiritually, their church home. When they become young adults, their church should make every effort to bring them to a personal commitment to Christ through special events that present knowing Christ personally, calling for an intimate relationship with him.

Other possible applications of this model include church school resources. Teachers should note the holistic approach of this model, and build resources accordingly. Teaching materials should strengthen the embeddedness situation: the home, the school, and the congregation. Values education courses in the public school systems could also offer the holistic approach to growth and reveal the effect of embeddedment. What is meaningful? What does our society value? How does that affect the embeddedness each child relates to and draws security from for growth? All faith gifts refer to that which society values, but sadly, these values are often given mere lip service, only confusing the child. Children are shown a double standard that seriously affects their ability to reach out for the truth.

This view of Life as gift motivates growth in faith. The gifts reach us through other people around us with an open spirit. Gifts reach us in many ways, and are similar to the Biblical gifts of the Spirit, and the spiritual fruits that develop in a life walked with the Spirit. The fruits of the Spirit are found in Galatians 5:22. A comparison between them and the faith gifts in the Spiral Faith Model is interesting. The Spiral Faith Model was not based on these spiritual gifts as such, but they have obviously greatly influenced an understanding of faith gifts in each spiral.

Fruits of the Spirit	**Faith Gifts**
love	trust
joy	joy
peace	O.K. ness
patience	gospel (people's stories)
kindness	forgiveness
goodness	acceptance of difference
faithfulness	love
humility	caring
self-control	acceptance of limits
	letting go
	hope
	peace

Can we speak of the gifts of the Spirit corresponding to natural growth through the life cycle? Are they confined to the baptism of the Spirit, and subsequent growth in faith, or are they part of the life-long growth process? The power of such an outpouring of God's grace during a particular experience in a person's life is not denied here, but the Spirit deals with each life as it unfolds. Growth in the Spirit depends on openness to gifts and the appropriation of them in life bearing fruit. The Spiral Faith Model delineates maximum openness during a particular spiral in the life cycle; this includes openness to the Spirit in the specific response indicated. This model does not limit God's gifts in any way — it is human openness (or lack of it) that limits them.

Finally, what is the relation between Biblical revelation and growth in faith through the life cycle? Does the Spiral Faith Model deny the place of revelation as God's direct act in a person's life? Is there a spiritual encounter that reveals truth directly, or through scripture, or through prayer? Does God break in at a particular time, or is revelation in progress throughout the life cycle? Surely it has to be both, or we limit God!

Kenneth Leech, writing in *Soul Friend*, traces the faith journey as "The practice of Christian Spirituality," the book's subtitle. The goal of the spiritual journey is union with God, that is, seeing God face to face (Revelation 22:4). This is the ultimate goal of the spirit that seeks its end in its beginning with God. Leech points out that there cannot be an experience of union with God without a radical transformation of consciousness in which there is a transcendence of the ego, and an entering into God-consciousness.[1]

The New Testament distinguishes between the beginning of the Christian life and the maturity, or perfection, of that life, meaning that the person's completion is in seeing God, being in union with God (Philippians 1:6, 3:12). Calling the end of the faith journey "maturity," or "perfection," is a poor process term. Wholeness, or completion, is a better term. Appropriating faith gifts helps to complete a person's life as each spiral unfolds.

What is it like to go through life with little faith? Is it a world devoid of colour? I once dreamed of that kind of world. I went through a hole in a sand wall into a world the colour of buff, looking for a friend. The windows were covered with a very flimsy material like gauze, and inside everyone was lying still holding a fetal position. It was terrible. Where was my friend? Was I too late? As I looked around something like a hose from a vacuum cleaner came through the window and started to suck up everything in the room. It came at me. I was horrified and barely had the strength to drag it off my arm. It tried to suck the life out of me! I escaped wishing I could do something to help in that terrible world. Will this be our world in time? Was it a dream of a post-nuclear world, or what? Faith is meaning-making. So, what is life all about . . . in vivid colour?

FOOTNOTES

[1]Kenneth Leech, *Soul Friend. The Practice of Christian Spirituality* (San Francisco: Harper & Row, 1980), p. 158.

Stage Theory

Stage theory forms the base from which all developmental concepts have grown, including growth in faith. In stage theory growth is developmental in the sense that a person moves through stages in a sequential pattern. In each stage there are developmental tasks to accomplish: success in these tasks secures happiness; failure in them negates growth in the next stage. For example, the baby experiences a balance between trust and mistrust in the first few months of life, which affects all he or she does from then on.

The best known of stage theorists, Erik Erikson, published an essay in the '50s outlining his "Eight Stages of Man" in the book *Childhood and Society*. These eight stages have become the basis of all subsequent stage theory presentations. Over the years Erikson has not made much change in the formation of each stage. Here is a table of Erikson's eight stages, showing their psychosocial tasks as the favourable/unfavourable resolution of attitude in each stage.

		Favourable Resolution	Unfavourable Resolution
Stage	Period	Attitude	Attitude
1	Early infancy	Trust	Mistrust
2	Late infancy	Autonomy	Shame/doubt
3	Early Childhood	Initiative	Guilt
4	Middle Childhood	Industry	Inferiority
5	Adolescence	Identity	Identity confusion
6	Early adulthood	Intimacy	Isolation
7	Middle adulthood	Generativety	Stagnation
8	Late adulthood	Ego integrity	Despair[1]

For an explanation of Erikson's theory we could turn to several writers, but the summary in the "Eriksonian Measure of Psychological Development," by Gwen A. Hawley is especially helpful:

> There is an adjustment needed in each stage, in the form of the resolution of a conflict between alternative attitudes. These attitudes make up the personality. They are formed through the resolving of the tension in a favorable or unfavorable manner depending on which of the two stage attitudes predominates. Their resolution can mean the development of a certain moral virtue. Though not restricted to any age, a particular crises seems to predominate at a certain age."[2]

Erikson makes several assumptions in his theory. Hawley's list of these assumptions is worth noting as it will help the reader understand stage theory:

Each attitude exists in some form from the beginning to the end of life.

Each stage attitude is related to all others.

The attitudes depend on the proper development in the proper sequence of all others.

The attitudes are expressed in polarities suggesting their opposition as well as the nature of a positive or negative resolution of a stage crises.

No stage conflict is resolved once for all. (Unresolved tensions crop up in later stages.)

Progression through stages varies in tempo and intensity.

The successful or unsuccessful resolution of the crises determines the overall health of the personality.

Personality is shaped by the manner in which the stage crises are resolved.[3]

It bothers some people that each stage is marked by a crisis, but crisis here means a turning point. It can be a helpful crisis, even though it is usually marked by a feeling of vulnerability. There is the potential in such a crisis to progress or fall back, in other words, it holds potential for growth. The tension at each stage can be resolved in a favourable or unfavourable way.

Another early influence on stage theorists was Robert Havighurst. Writing in the '40s, Havighurst was the first to introduce what he called the developmental task in his book, *Developmental Tasks in Education*. The *Westminster Dictionary* defines a developmental task as "a task that arises at or about a certain period in the life of an individual, successful achievement of which leads to happiness and to success with later tasks, while failure leads to unhappiness in the individual, disapproval by society and difficulty with later tasks."[4] Havighurst has identified various tasks for each age span from infancy to late maturity. These tasks arise from three influences: physical maturation, cultural pressures, and individual values.

For further reading focusing on developmental tasks there is Barbara M. and Philip R. Newman's book, *Development Through Life: A Psychological Approach.*[5] This is a survey of human development in the life cycle, focusing on the psychosocial tasks and crisis resolution for each major stage.

The idea that there are certain developmental tasks in each of the stages pertains to growth in faith. What would the faith task be in each stage? Or can we even talk in these terms, using concepts from developmental theory?

During a particular stage a person is more open to achieving a certain task which would make further development of that and other tasks in succeeding stages easier. This openness is the idea of the teachable moment: that certain tasks are more suitable in a certain stage, and easier to learn then. Teachable moments are related to experience and biological maturation, and are also influenced by culture and values. All teachable moments can be helpful in understanding openness to growth, especially to growth in faith. Is there a time when a person is more open to certain faith *tasks* during a certain stage or is it more appropriate to talk about openness to faith *gifts* in each stage?

Everything we experience can teach us something about life's meaning. How a person reacts to the apparent conflicts within available choices can turn the self inward or outward to others. In this searching for balance, a faith response can be strengthened or weakened. If the person turns outward from self there is growth in faith; putting it another way, there is a move towards self-transcendence. If a person turns inward, away from other people, the reverse is true. When choices are positive, faithing becomes a response to the experiences of life in a self-transcendent mode, taking a person beyond self.

In stage theory each stage is marked by crisis. This is the turning point: it can be a growth crisis or it can provoke shut-down, and is usually marked by a feeling of vulnerability. Stage theorists say that such crises are predictable; they can identify various transitions, and how each one can last anywhere from six months to several years. This approach tends to say that all humans walk similar paths, and that much of what happens within a certain stage is predictable. Whether this predictability applies to growth in faith is questionable. However, there are similarities in everyone's response to crisis, in resolving or avoiding it, so the typical route in the faith journey can probably be documented by research.

We turn now to the work of researchers in faith development, among whom James Fowler has set the standard. Writing in the early 1980's, Fowler follows a school of thought based on Jean Piaget and Lawrence Kohlberg. These men wrote largely in the area of cognitive development, influencing Fowler so that he seems to be defining faith as mental activity in the field of knowing and thinking. Following the research of Piaget, he makes the assumption that the mind works in an orderly fashion. Information is organized by the mind, and this "knowing" is regulated in given ways by developmental tasks at any particular point, or stage, in a person's life. Kohlberg has applied Piaget's principles to his developmental model for moral judgement. At what stage or age, for instance, does a child know right from wrong? Fowler has used Kohlberg's moral stage theory and worked out a pattern, or set of stages for faith development. Based on ten years of research and interviews with over 500 persons, his is the first major organization of theological concepts within the framework of the human life cycle.

Fowler's Stages of Faith Development

Stage 1:   Intuitive–Projective Faith
           Young children up to about age seven reflect the visible faith of their parents.
           (Transition: Emergence of concrete thinking, i.e., God is an "old man" in the sky.)

Stage 2:   Mythic–Literal Faith
           In later childhood the person takes on beliefs of persons other than parents, through story, drama, etc., without reflecting on them.
           (Transition: Contradictions between stories.)

Stage 3:   Synthetic–Conventional Faith
           Early teens conform to the "gang." Faith begins to
           synthesize life's increasing complexity. When
           adults are strongly influenced by peers they are in
           Stage 3.
           (Transition: A synthesis of values and information is
           basic for identity and outlook.)

Stage 4:   Individual–Reflective Faith
           In the late teens and early adulthood the focus is
           on adult responsibility, on a person's own commit-
           ments and beliefs. Doubting, questioning, and re-
           jecting traditional assumptions are a part of Stage
           4. This is the period in which one's own individual
           values are developed.
           (Transition: A move towards seeing one's life as part
           of the whole.)

Stage: 5   Conjunctive Faith
           A mature faith stage seldom found before age 30
           (and often never reached). This stage incorporates
           the integrity of positions other than one's own, and
           responds to an identification beyond race, class, or
           ideological boundaries. Stage five adults integrate
           traditional positions, their own doubts, and the
           views of others into a meaningful whole.
           (Transition: As the next stage is a true reflection of
           what the divine wills, it is achieved only by grace, or
           as vocation in answer to life's call.)

Stage 6:   Universalizing Faith
           Faith is a universal in which the individual
           identifies beyond self with God (divine being) as a
           felt reality.[6]

   Fowler's style of writing is hard to follow. Many of his concepts are difficult and impossible to remember, but his framework has inspired others to try formulating a simpler model.

Fowler also sees "faith" as active, a verb. Faith is not something that one does or does not have, but rather is a process of becoming. This process is continual growth through stages that are "hierarchical" (increasingly complex and quantitative), "sequential" (they appear one after the other in the life span), and "invariant" (they follow the same order for all persons).

Fowler's work has been severely criticized for several reasons, especially for applying cognitive theories to faith development. Is faith only mental "knowing"? Thomas A. Droege in his book, *Faith Passages and Patterns*, says that "Faith-knowing is faith seeking understanding." He goes on to connect this knowing with the images, faith-form stories, concepts, and doctrines that are the receptacles of this knowledge.[7] As faith involves the whole person, we must ask, what about the emotions, the feelings, the present-day experiences? How do these affect development, especially growth in faith?

Regardless of all criticism, Fowler's contribution to faith development needs to be recognized. He has set the stage for approaching an understanding of growth in faith throughout the life cycle. Even though understanding faith as cognitive knowledge is much too limiting, mental knowing is certainly a part of faith. Can stage theory really be applied to faith? Is faith development sequential, hierarchical, and invariant? The Spiral Faith Model offers a far more flexible way of looking at growth in faith; it includes mental, psychological, social, and spiritual concepts without an emphasis on hierarchical growth, as spirals can go up and down.

Another writer who has influenced the Spiral Faith Model is Robert Kegan. In his book, *The Evolving Self*, Kegan uses a cyclic model to depict growth. Kegan's model also focuses on the idea of embeddedment within the psychosocial factors of each stage, making for a sense of security in a person's development.[8] The Spiral Faith Model has taken note of this concept of embeddedment and points out the relational factors that allow a person to be secure and open in facing faith's task, the appropriation of faith gifts.

As a colleague of Carol Gilligan, Kegan noted the criticism Gilligan made of the developmental research theories and incorporated some of her insights into his book. Carol Gilligan in *In A Different Voice: Psychological Theory and Women's Development*[9] is highly critical of stage theory for imposing on women a male model of development. The omission of the experience of women has seriously affected Erikson's stage development theory between stages four to six. Women's development is formed mainly through relationship, not just through autonomy. Autonomy, initiative, industry are separation terms, reflecting masculine independence. Using Gilligan's insights, Kegan has added another stage to Erikson's model, the Interpersonal. This is more in line with the development of women, who form their identity through "a web of connectedness," that is, through relationships. This emphasis on growth through relationship is incorporated into the Spiral Faith Model from Spiral 5 onwards.

When growth's direction is towards independence, it affects the identity issue. A woman's identity is formed through her relationships (for instance, as mother, spouse, boss). This is not to say that she functions merely as someone's shadow, but that a woman's world view is constructed in terms of relationship. This has often meant that a woman holds off formation of an identity until a later stage. Unfortunately, concern for relationship tends to be devalued by men and regarded as a "weakness," but this is beginning to change.

How do concerns about relationship affect growth in faith? Relationships form the embeddedness out of which a person reaches for growth. Supportive people call a person out of self to respond and thereby grow. Sociologists, have emphasized that growth has more dimensions than the cognitive, competitive, and moral. The Spiral Faith Model, fancy to death, acknowledges that the invitation to faith involves a reaching out toward others, but that each person will move toward self-transcendence in a unique way.

FOOTNOTES

[1] Erik Erikson, *Childhood and Society* (New York: Norton, 1950).

[2] Reproduced by special permission of the publisher, Psychological Assessment Resources, Inc., 16102 North Florida Avenue, Lutz, Florida 33549, from *The Eriksonian Measure of Psychosocial Development* by Gwen Hawley. Copyright 1986. Further reproduction is prohibited without permission from PAR, Inc.

[3] *Ibid.*

[4] Robert J. Havighurst, *Developmental Tasks and Education*, Third Edition (New York: Longman, 1972). Reprinted by permission of the publisher.

[5] Barbara M. and Philip R. Newman, *Developmental through Life: A Psychological Approach* (Homewood, Ill: Dorsey Press, 1979).

[6] Compiled by and used with permission from Dr. Kenneth Stokes, Executive Director of Adult Faith Resources.

[7] Thomas A. Droege, *Faith Passages and Patterns* (Philadelphia: Fortress Press, 1983), p. 13.

[8] Robert Kegan, *The Evolving Self: Problem and Process in Development* (Cambridge: Harvard University Press, 1982), p. 165.

[9] Carol Gilligan, *In A Different Voice: Psychological Theory and Women's Development* (Cambridge: Harvard University Press, 1982).

BIBLIOGRAPHY

Capps, Donald. *Life Cycle Theory and Pastoral Care.* Philadelphia: Fortress Press, 1983.

This volume from the series Theology and Pastoral Care takes the life cycle as its focus, and explores a model consisting of three important dimensions.

Conn, Joann Wolski, Ed. *Women's Spritiuality: Resources for Christian Development.* New York: Paulist Press, 1986.

An anthology of edited selections from feminist psychology and classic spirituality.

Droege, Thomas A. *Faith Passages and Patterns.* Philadelphia: Fortress Press, 1983.

The theories of Erikson and Fowler are blended with Biblical reflection in a practical focus for individuals.

Erikson, Erik H. *Childhood and Society.* New York: Norton, 1950.

An early book by Erikson in which he sets out the "Eight Stages of Man."

Fowler, James W. *Stages of Faith.* San Francisco: Harper & Row, 1981.

Fowler develops his stage theory of Faith Development and details the research that underlies it.

_____. *Becoming Adult, Becoming Christian: Adult Development and Christian Faith.* San Francisco: Harper & Row, 1984.

Fowler explores in more detail and expands his stage theory of Faith Development for adults with a conscious Christian focus.

Gilligan, Carol. *In a Different Voice: Psychological Theory and Women's Development.* Cambridge: Harvard University Press, 1982.

Gilligan takes a strong feminist stand in arguing for an understanding of the unique differences between women's and men's patterns of development.

Grant, W. Harold, Thompson, Magdala, and Clarke, Thomas E. *From Image to Likeness: A Jungian Path in the Gospel Journey.* New York: Paulist Press, 1983.

This book correlates Jungian types with Gospel themes and Christian values and links it with the Myers-Briggs Type Indicator.

Groeschel, Benedict J. *Spiritual Passages: The Psychology of Spiritual Development.* New York: Crossroad, 1984.

A well balanced and stimulating integration of psychology and spirituality for those interested in their spiritual journey.

Hamilton, Neill Q. *Maturing in the Christian Life: A Pastor's Guide.* Philadelphia: The Geneva Press, 1984.

A good book for busy pastors interested in Christian maturity.

Havighurst, Robert J. *Developmental Tasks in Education.* New York: David McKay, 1972.

Havighurst developed the concept of developmental tasks; since then it has become widely accepted in the field of human development.

Kegan, Robert. *The Evolving Self: Problem and Process in Human Development.* Cambridge: Harvard University Press, 1982.

Kegan used the concept of development and illustrated various growth periods with spirals. He pointed out the social embeddedment necessary for growth.

Kidd, J. R. *How Adults Learn.* New York: Association Press, 1959.

This book is a basic one for adult education. It deals with the process of adult learning and has influenced later writing on the subject.

Kolbenschlag, Madonna. *Kiss Sleeping Beauty Good-bye: Breaking the Spell of Feminine Myths and Models.* New York: Doubleday and Co., 1979.

This book deals with the myths and fairy tales that have shaped women's lives and directed their behaviour.

Levinson, Daniel J. *The Seasons of a Man's Life.* New York: Alfred Knopf, 1978.

A description of research related to the developmental cycle of men, with particular reference to the "mid-life transition."

Leech, Kenneth. *Soul Friend.* "The Practice of Christian Spirituality." San Francisco: Harper & Row, 1977.

Leech combines his knowledge of Christian spirituality with a good understanding of psychological growth.

Lyon, K. Brynoff. *Toward a Practical Theology of Aging.* Philadelphia: Fortress Press, 1985.

From the series *Theology and Pastoral Care*, this volume considers the relationship of human fulfillment and aging in the context of pastoral care.

Maitland, David J. *Looking Both Ways: A Theology for Mid-life.* Altanta: John Knox Press, 1985.

A poignant yet theologically grounded exploration of mid-life and its opportunities for growth from a conscious Christian perspective.

McCoy, V. R., Ryan, C. and Lichtenberg, J.W. *The Adult Life Cycle Training Manual and Reader.* Lawrence, (Kansas): Adult Life Resource Center, University of Kansas, 1978.

A variety of readings and group exercises related to the adult life cycle, with particular emphasis on mid-life.

McCullough, Charles. *Heads of Heaven, Feet of Clay: Ideas and Stories for Adult Faith Education.* New York: Pilgrim Press, 1983.

Theories of human development are augmented by several useful designs for adult faith education in the church setting.

Miller, Jean Baker. *Toward a New Psychology of Women.* Boston: Beacon Press, 1976.

Miller tries to help women see that authenticity and subordination are incompatible. Women need to build up their own self-image.

Neugarten, Bernice L., Ed. *Middle Age and Aging*. Chicago: the University of Chicago Press, 1968.

Undoubtedly the most comprehensive review of research on middle age available from one of the outstanding scholars in the field.

Newman, Barbara M., and Newman, Philip R. *Development Through Life: A Psychological Approach*. Homewood, Ill.: Dorsey Press, 1979.

A survey of human development in the life cycle, focusing on psychosocial crises of each major stage.

Powers, Bruce P. *Growing Faith*. Nashville: Boardman Press, 1982.

Faith development theory's practical implications are explored and illustrated; learning activities are included.

Sheehy, Gail. *Passages: Predictable Crises of Adult Life*. New York: E. P. Dutton, 1976.

Though erudite, this author is highly readable and her thoughts are well illustrated.

Spencer, Anita Louise. *Seasons; Women's Search for Self Through Life's Stages*. Ramsey, NJ: Paulist Press, 1982.

Using the seasons of the year, the author suggests feminine alternatives to Levinson's male-oriented concepts.

Stokes, Kenneth, Ed. *Faith Development in the Adult Life Cycle*. New York: William H. Sadlier, 1982.

Part of a major study seeking to determine relationships between chronological periods of adulthood and the individual's faith attitudes.

Van Kaam, Adrian. *The Transcendent Self: The Formative Spirituality of Middle, Early and Later Years of Life*. Denville: Dimension Books, 1979.

The dynamics of transcendence as one of the fundamental aspects of personal and spiritual formation.

Whitehead, Evelyn E., and Whitehead, James D. *Christian Life Pattern: The Psychological Challenges and Religious Invitations of Adult Life*. New York:: Doubleday and Co., 1979.

The Whiteheads explore the relationship between Erikson's adult stages and faith development.

——————————. *Seasons of Strength: New Visions of Adult Christian Maturing*. New York: Doubleday & Co., 1984.

The authors are guided by two ideas: vocation and virtue in the Christian maturing of adults. They focus on the need to renew patterns of power, confidence, and loss, which shape maturity.

Washbourn, Penelope. *Becoming Woman: The Quest for Wholeness in Female Experience*. San Francisco: Harper & Row, 1977.

Washbourn examines ten critical points in the life of a woman. This was the first full-length feminist theology to explore the personal and spiritual questions implicit in the female life cycle.